THE BIBLE
IN ITS CONTEXT

How to improve your study of the Scriptures

Dr. Craig Keener

First Fruits Press,
Wilmore, KY
c2024

ISBN: **9781648172359**
The Bible in its context : how to improve your study of the Scriptures
Craig Keener
First Fruits Press, ©2024

Digital version at https://place.asburyseminary.edu/academicbooks/52/

For all other uses, contact:
First Fruits Press
B.L. Fisher Library
Asbury Theological Seminary
204 N. Lexington Ave.
Wilmore, KY 40390
http://place.asburyseminary.edu/firstfruits

Keener, Craig S., 1960-
    The Bible in its context : how to improve your study of the Scriptures / Craig
    Keener. – Wilmore, Kentucky : First Fruits Press, ©2024.

    308 pages ; cm.

    ISBN: 9781648172359 (paperback)
    ISBN: 9781648172366 (uPDF)
    ISBN: 9781648172373 (Mobi)
    OCLC: 1442930039

    1. Bible--Hermeneutics. 2. Bible--Criticism, interpretation, etc. 3. Bible--Study and
teaching. 4. Bible--History of contemporary events. 5. Bible--History of Biblical
events. I. Title.

BS476.K43 2024   220.601

Cover design by Amanda Kessinger

asburyseminary.edu
800.2ASBURY
204 North Lexington Avenue
Wilmore, Kentucky 40390

First Fruits
THE ACADEMIC OPEN PRESS OF ASBURY SEMINARY

First Fruits Press
The Academic Open Press of Asbury Theological Seminary
204 N. Lexington Ave., Wilmore, KY 40390
859-858-2236
first.fruits@asburyseminary.edu
asbury.to/firstfruits

Contents

Introduction

In Josiah's day the book of the law was found in the temple, and Josiah's humble response to its demands changed his generation. Jesus later confronted religious teachers of His day who, for all their attention to the law, had often buried it beneath their religious traditions. Numerous monastic orders through the Middle Ages kept finding the church (or earlier orders) corrupt and far from the apostolic message, and summoned them back to it. John Wycliffe, a Bible professor at Oxford, challenged the church hierarchy of his day. After he lost his position, he began sending his students out with translations of Scripture to preach in the countryside. Although England suppressed his work, it lay under the surface, ready to blossom again in the English Reformation a century later. Luther was a Bible professor who challenged the church hierarchy's exploitation of the peasants, calling the church back to the Scriptures (other Reformers had the same emphasis, some seeking to take the matter even further than Luther). When many Lutherans became complacent in their faith, Philipp Jakob Spener, a university professor, helped stir the Pietist movement with his Bible teaching, summoning people back to living the Scriptures.

Throughout history, many of the major revival movements came as people turned back to the Bible, allowing it to challenge them to hear God's message afresh in their generation. The church in much of the world today needs to return to the Bible no less, seeking from God a fresh wind of the Spirit to challenge many of the claims made in the name of God, His word, or His Spirit. May we pray for such an awakening, search the Scriptures ourselves, and become God's agents in spreading His message.

I arrange this course from the most basic principles to the more complex. Some students may find principles like "context" too basic and may wish to skip ahead. Before they do so, I encourage them to sample the context examples; many will be surprised how many songs, sermons, and popular sayings have taken texts out of their context. In other words, it is one thing to affirm that we believe in context; it is quite another to practice that skill consistently. I have supplied concrete examples to help us grapple with that reality and encourage us to apply our "belief" in context more rigorously. Context is essential because that is the way God inspired the Bible—not with random, isolated verses but with a continuous flow of thought to which those verses contribute.

Some issues of interpretation perhaps should go without saying, but I will treat them briefly in the introduction, because some Christians also fail to apply these in practice. The central goal of studying God's Word is to know God better, and the better we know Him, the better we will understand His Word. Because God gave us the Bible as a written book that contains much history, He does expect us to use literary and historical principles when we study it. But it is also a record of the message of God's heart to His people, so we dare not approach it as merely a matter of intellectual interest or curiosity. Those who become "experts" from a purely intellectual or even religious standpoint can become like the scribes who opposed our Lord Jesus. We must remember that this book, unlike normal books, has the right to make moral demands on our lives. We do not become "experts" who show off our knowledge. We must humble ourselves before the God of Scripture.

The fear of the Lord is the beginning of wisdom and knowledge (Prov 1:7; 9:10). Our human tendency is to read into Scripture whatever we want to find there, whether to justify our behavior or to confirm what we have already been taught by our church, our tradition, or by other teachers we look up to. Slaveholders tried to justify their behavior from the Bible; many cults justify their doctrines from the Bible; but sometimes we Christians do the same things. If we fear God, we will want to hear only what His Word teaches us, and hear it as accurately as possible.

We must also be willing to obey God once we hear Him. James tells us that if we want wisdom we (like Solomon) should ask for it (1:5). But we need to ask in faith, he insists (1:6), and he later explains that *real* faith is faith that is ready to live according to God's demands (2:14-26). If we really pray for God to teach us the Bible (and we should; see Ps 119!), we must pray with the kind of faith that is ready to embrace what we find in the Bible. We must embrace what we find there even if it is unpopular, even if it gets us in trouble, and even if it challenges the way we live. That is a high price, but it comes with a benefit: the excitement of often finding fresh, new discoveries, rather than simply hearing what we expected to hear.

Studying God's Word with an open and yearning heart is one way that we express our love for God. God's chief command to Israel was His declaration that He is one (Deut 6:4), hence there is no room for idols. Therefore, He admonished His people to love Him alone, with an undivided heart and one's whole being (Deut 6:5). Those who love God in this way will talk of His Word all the time, everywhere, with everyone (Deut 6:6-9). If God is really first in our lives, then His Word will be central to us, and consume us.

Sometimes people miss the heart of God's Word. The Pharisees debated about details but missed the bigger picture of God's heart of justice, mercy and faithfulness (what Jesus calls, "the weightier matters of the law," Matt 23:23); in the familiar English figure of speech, they missed the forest for the trees. All of Scripture is God's Word, but some parts teach us more directly about God's character than others (for example, we learn more directly from God's revelation to Moses in Ex 33—34 than from rituals in Leviticus). Sometimes we may even hear God wrongly when we read the Bible, simply because our background predisposes us to think of God as always harsh or always indulgent.

Where do we look to find the central revelation of God's character (Jesus' "weightier matters") that helps us rightly apply the rest of God's Word? God revealed His law to Israel, but both Old Testament prophets and the New Testament show that some aspects of that law applied directly only to ancient Israel in a particular time (though we can all learn from its eternal principles). The prophets offered dynamic applications of the law based on knowing God's heart. But God has most fully revealed His heart and His Word by sending us Jesus; when His Word became flesh, He revealed God's heart (Jn 1:1-18). When Moses received the law on Mount Sinai, he saw some of God's glory, some of His character of grace and truth; but no one could see God fully and live (Ex 33:18-20; 34:6).

In the Word become flesh, however, God revealed His glorious grace and truth fully (Jn 1:14, 17); now the unseen God has been fully revealed in Jesus Christ (Jn 1:18; 14:9).

In this study, we will look further at context; whole-book context; background; and specific principles for understanding specific kinds of writings in the Bible (such as psalms, proverbs, laws, and prophecies. These are essential principles for learning what God was saying to the first readers, a necessary step in hearing how to apply God's message today. But we still need God's Spirit to guide us in how to apply His message to our own lives, to the church today, and to our world. There is more than one way to hear God's voice (we hear Him, for example, in prayer), but it is through study of Scripture that we learn to recognize His voice accurately when He speaks to us in other ways. Paul warns that we both "know in part and prophesy in part" (1 Cor 13:9). That is why it is good for us to depend on both Scripture and the Spirit to help us hear accurately. But the Spirit will not truly say something that contradicts what He already inspired Scripture to say (the way He gave it to us, in context).

Please note: many ideas in the genre parts of this manual closely follow Gordon Fee and Douglas Stuart's *How to Read the Bible for All Its Worth* (Zondervan); I am especially indebted to their work on psalms and epistles. Most of the rest, however, began especially from inductively grappling with the Bible itself over many years, and then with the ancient sources that reveal the world of the Bible.

This manual may be shared freely but only on the condition that it is always free and that these credits remain. (It is "shareware" for public use, like a sermon, originally designed for use with students in Nigeria, not for traditional publication or financial remuneration.) The "background" illustrations can be found in much greater detail in Craig Keener's (i.e., my) *IVP Bible Background Commentary: New Testament* (Downers Grove, IL: InterVarsity, 1993, with about a quarter of a million in print)

—Dr. Craig Keener

Chapter 1
Context, Context, Context!

Have you ever been quoted out of context? Sometimes people quote something you said, but by ignoring the context of what you said they can claim that you said something different—sometimes exactly the opposite of what you actually meant! We often make this same mistake with the Bible. That is how cults like Jehovah's Witnesses or Mormons use the Bible to defend their unbiblical teachings.

One of the most important resources for understanding the Bible is in the Bible itself: context. Some readers want to skip immediately to verses elsewhere in the Bible. (Sometimes they do this by using references in their Bible's margins; yet these were added by editors, and are not part of the Bible itself.) Unfortunately, we can make the Bible say almost anything by combining different verses; even verses that sound similar may in context address quite different topics. Using this method, one would think that "one is justified by faith without works" (Rom 3:28) and "one is justified by works, and not by faith alone"

(James 2:24) contradict each other. By contrast, each passage makes sense in a special way if we read it in its context: the flow of thought from what comes before and after the passage we are studying. In context, James and Paul mean something quite different by "faith." Both affirm that a person is made right before God only by a sort of genuine faith that is expressed in a fairly consistent life of obedience (see our discussion below).

If we ignore context, we will almost always misunderstand what we read in the Bible. Advanced students may wish to skip to later chapters of the book, but because many students assume that they have understand context better than they actually do, we would urge readers to at least sample the next chapter before moving further.

The Importance of Context

Context is the way God gave us the Bible, one book at a time. The first readers of Mark could not flip over to Revelation to help them understand Mark; Revelation had not been written yet. The first readers of Galatians did not have a copy of the letter Paul wrote to Rome to help them understand it. These first readers did share some common information with the author outside the book they received. In this manual we call this shared information "background": some knowledge of the culture, earlier biblical history, and so on. But they had, most importantly, the individual book of the Bible that was in front of them. Therefore we can be confident that the writers of the Bible included enough within each book of the Bible to help the readers understand that book of the Bible without referring to information they lacked. For that reason, context is the most important academic key to Bible interpretation. (Background, what the writer could take for granted, is also important; we will return to that subject in a later chapter.)

Often popular ministers today quote various isolated verses they have memorized, even though this means that they will usually leave 99% of the Bible's verses unpreached. One seemingly well-educated person told a Bible teacher that she thought the purpose of having a Bible was to look up the verses the minister quoted in church! But the Bible is not a collection of people's favorite verses with a lot of blank space in between. Using verses out of context one could "prove" almost anything about God or justify almost any kind of behavior--as history testifies. But in the Bible God revealed Himself in His acts in history, through the inspired records of those acts and the inspired wisdom of His servants addressing specific situations.

People in my culture value everything "instant": "instant" mashed potatoes; fast food; and so forth. Similarly, we too often take short-cuts to understanding the Bible by quoting random verses or assuming that others who taught us have understood them correctly. When we do so, we fail to be *diligent* in seeking God's Word (Prov 2:2-5; 4:7; 8:17; 2 Tim 2:15). One prominent minister in the U.S., Jim Bakker, was so busy with his ministry to millions of people that he did not have time to study Scripture carefully in context. He trusted that his friends whose teachings he helped promote surely had done so. Later, when his ministry collapsed, he spent many hours honestly searching the Scriptures and realized to his horror that on some points Jesus' teachings, understood in context, meant the exact opposite of what he and his friends had been teaching! It is never safe to simply depend on what someone else claims that God says (1 Kgs 13:15-26).

I discovered this for myself when, as a young Christian, I began reading 40 chapters of the Bible a day (enough to finish the New Testament every week or the Bible every month). I was shocked to discover how much Scripture I had essentially ignored between the verses I had memorized, and how carefully the intervening text connected those verses. I had been missing so much, simply using the Bible to defend what I already believed! After one begins reading the Bible a book at a time, one quickly recognizes that verses isolated from their context nearly always mean something different when read in context. We cannot, in fact, even pretend to make sense of most verses without reading their context. Isolating verses from their context disrespects the authority of Scripture because this method of interpretation cannot be consistently applied to the whole of Scripture. It picks verses that seem to make sense on their own, but most of the rest of the Bible is left over when it is done, incapable of being used the same way. Preaching and teaching the Bible the way it invites us to interpret it—in its original context--both explains the Bible accurately and provides our hearers a good example how they can learn the Bible better for themselves.

If we read any other book, we would not simply take an isolated statement in the middle of the book and ignore the surrounding statements that help us understand the reason for that statement. If we hand a storybook to a child already learning how to read, the child would probably start reading at the beginning. That people so often read the Bible out of context (I will offer examples below) is not because it comes naturally to us, but because we have been *taught* the wrong way by frequent example. Without disrespecting those who have done the best they could without understanding the principle of context, we must now avail ourselves of the chance to begin teaching the next generation the right way to interpret the Bible.

Many contradictions some readers claim to find in the Bible arise simply from ignoring the context of the passages they cite, jumping from one text to another without taking the time to first understand each text on its own terms. To develop an example offered above, when Paul says that a person is justified by faith without works (Rom 3:28), his context makes it clear that he defines faith as something more than passive assent to a viewpoint; he defines it as a conviction that Christ is our salvation, a conviction on which one actively stakes one's life (Rom 1:5). James declares that one cannot be justified by faith without works (James 2:14)—because he uses the word "faith" to mean mere assent that something is true (2:19), he demands that such assent be actively demonstrated by obedience to show that it is genuine (2:18). In other words, James and Paul use the word "faith" differently, but do not contradict one another on the level of meaning. If we ignore context and merely connect different verses on the basis of similar wording, we will come up with contradictions in the Bible that the original writers would never have imagined.

Levels of Context

Most of us agree that we should read the Bible in context, but how far should we read in the context? Is it sufficient merely to read the verse before and the verse after the one we are quoting? Or should we be familiar with the paragraphs before and after? Or should we be familiar with the entire book of the Bible in which the passage occurs? While in practice the answer to this question depends to some extent on the part of the Bible we are studying (context is much shorter in Proverbs than in Genesis or 2 Corinthians), as a general rule we should think of each passage both in its immediate context and in the context of the entire book of the Bible in which it appears.

Many Bible teachers have wisely spoken of various levels of context for any text. First, most texts have an immediate context in the paragraph or paragraphs surrounding them. Second, we can look at the context of the entire book of the Bible in which they appear, the one unit of text we can be sure the first writers expected the first readers to have in front of them. Third, we sometimes need to look at the whole context of that writer's teaching. For instance, though the Corinthians could not consult Paul's letter to the Galatians, they were familiar with a broader backdrop of his teaching than what we find in 1 Corinthians alone, because Paul taught them in person for eighteen months (Acts 18:11). Whatever we can learn about Paul's broader teaching may help us, provided we give *first* priority to what he tells his audience in the *particular* letter we are trying to understand.

Fourth, there is the context of shared information—the background that the original writer shared with his readers. Some of this background may be available for us in the Bible (for instance, Paul could expect many of his readers to know the Old Testament), but discovering background may also require extra research (though the first readers, who normally already knew it, could take it for granted). Finally, we can look at the context of God's entire revelation in the Bible. But this should be our final step, not our first one. Too often we want to explain one verse in light of another before we have really understood either verse in light of the immediate context in which they occur. As in the example of Romans and James above, a particular word or even phrase does not always carry the same meaning in every passage.

2 Timothy 3:16-17 declares that "every Scripture is profitable for doctrine, reproof, correction, and instruction in righteousness." Every Scripture communicates a meaning that is essential for the Church—as we have noted, there must be no "blank spaces" between our favorite verses. To apply this principle properly, however, we must determine what unit of the Bible Paul is talking about (what he means by "Scripture"). Paul obviously does not mean simply the individual words in the Bible; although individual words in the Bible are important because they contribute to the meaning of the text, an individual word, isolated by itself, could not communicate much meaning. (We need the word "and," but by itself it does not communicate any specifically and universally Christian meaning.) We must be sure to preach from the Bible, not from a dictionary! This is the danger of focusing on words by themselves rather than their larger function in sentences and passages.

Obvious as this principle is (that individual words are not the primary unit of meaning), readers of the Bible sometimes ignore it. I once read a devotion on Ezekiel 28 that focused on the word, "wisdom," and explained how wonderful wisdom was (based on its meaning in a Hebrew dictionary). The writer explained in detail the need for wisdom and never bothered to point out that Ezekiel 28 refers to the evil prince of Tyre, whose boasts of wisdom represent mere worldly wisdom. In other words, this expositor was not really preaching from Ezekiel 28, but from a Hebrew dictionary! Those who trace a meaning of a word through Scripture and then spend a whole sermon on their results may do better (provided they recognize the different ways the word may be used in different passages); sometimes we do need to study the meaning of words in this way. But those who preach from a list of verses where the word occurs still run the risk of preaching from a concordance rather than from the Bible itself. God did not inspire the Bible in concordance sequence; He inspired it book by book.

Even focusing on a verse read in its immediate context may be problematic (although less problematic), because that verse may not represent a full unit of thought. The verse references were not added to the Bible when it was being written, but only after it was finished; the unit of thought is often much larger than a verse, and it cannot make proper sense apart from its context. For example, that Jesus wept might be useful instruction for some people who think tears a sign of weakness. But remembering the context gives us a *more* generally useful principle. "Jesus wept" because He wept with friends who were suffering grief: this example teaches us that it is important to weep with those who weep, and that Jesus Himself cares for us enough to share our grief with us.

We may usually take a paragraph as a whole unit of thought, but even paragraphs often do not represent the complete unit of thought in the text. Paragraphs vary in length but we identify them as distinct paragraphs precisely because they are whole thoughts by themselves. Yet these thought-units often connect with other thought-units in such a way that it is difficult to separate them from surrounding thoughts. While most paragraphs will contain at least one nugget or principle, that nugget is sometimes too short to be used as the basis for a whole sermon by itself. As much as I prefer expository preaching (preaching from a paragraph or passage), some texts do not lend themselves easily to this approach.

For instance, when Paul bids farewell to his friends in Acts 20:36-38, their obvious love for one another (evidenced in their sad parting) yields a crucial nugget: We ought to have that kind of love for and commitment to one another in the body of Christ today. But we can articulate that principle more fully if we read these verses in light of Paul's preceding farewell speech (Acts 20:18-35). And we could find enough material on that passage for a lengthy sermon or Bible study—if we wish to stick to what the first readers of Acts had available—only if we traced that passage's theme of Christians' love for one another throughout the whole book in which it appears (e.g., 2:44-45; 4:32-35; 14:28; 28:14-15). Most congregations would like more than a single point to learn from, or at least more than a single illustration of the point! Commenting on unity in John 17:23 may be difficult to flesh out unless we see how John emphasizes unity in terms of loving one another (13:34-35) and the kinds of barriers unity must surmount (Jesus crosses a major ethnic barrier when he ministers to a Samaritan woman in John 4). Reading this verse about unity in the context of John's entire Gospel summons us to cross cultural and tribal barriers to love our fellow Christians.

One preaching professor in the U.S. told me that he was skeptical that all the Bible was God's Word; he doubted that one could preach from a passage like the one where David's servants brought him a concubine to keep him warm (1 Kgs 1:2-4). So I pointed out that these verses were part of a much larger context. After David sinned, God announced that judgment would come on his house even from those close to him (2 Sam 12:11). This was fulfilled in the revolt of Absalom, possibly David's eldest son after Amnon's death. But now another son of David, the next eldest after Absalom, is seeking to seize the throne (1 Kgs 1:5). The verses about David not being able to keep warm reveal how weak and susceptible he was to this new revolt; the mention of the concubine helps explain why Adonijah later merits death by asking to marry her (1 Kgs 2:21). To marry a concubine of the former king was to position oneself to become king (1 Kgs 2:22; cf. 2 Sam 16:21-22)--Adonijah still wants to overthrow Solomon's kingdom! Without having read the entire story, one may miss the purpose for the individual verses. But there is certainly a purpose for them, and the rest of the story would not make sense without them.

Ultimately, context extends beyond words, verses, and paragraphs to the entire structure of each book of the Bible. This is probably what Paul means when he says, "Every Scripture is inspired." The Greek word for "Scripture" here is *graphë*, which means "a writing." In most cases, each book of the Bible would be written on an individual scroll as an individual text; different books of the Bible were usually written as whole books to address different situations in ancient Israel or the church. Although these books often consisted of earlier materials (e.g., accounts about Jesus that circulated before writers of the Gospels wrote them down), we have them as whole units in our Bibles, and should read them as whole units. For instance, God gave us four Gospels instead of one because He wanted us to look at Jesus from more than one perspective. (Jesus was too great for merely one Gospel, with its distinctive emphasis, to teach us enough about Him.)

If we simply mix pieces from different Gospels without recognizing what is characteristic of each Gospel, we can miss the perspectives God wanted us to get from each one. While we could preach from an individual narrative in the Gospels and explain the text faithfully, we would do even better if we understood how that particular Bible story fit into the themes of that whole Gospel in which it appears.

In other cases, the book context is absolutely necessary, not just a nice addition. Paul's letter to the Romans, for instance, is a tight-knit argument; reading any passage in Romans without understanding the flow of logic in the whole book leaves us with only a piece of an argument. Admittedly many people read Romans this way, but because Romans is so tightly connected, Romans makes a far less immediately edifying Bible study passage-by-passage than Mark does. We need to know that all people have sinned (Rom 1—3), but one could easily spend many weeks analyzing that part of Romans before getting to justification by faith or power to live a righteous life. In Mark, by contrast, one comes up with new issues for study in nearly every paragraph, and a Bible study group could easily take a passage or chapter every week without feeling like they would not understand the writer's point for a few more weeks. Paul wrote Romans as a letter to be read as a tight-knit argument, all at once! Even Mark's first audience probably read his Gospel the entire way through in one sitting; it functions as a united account, foreshadowing Jesus' impending death and resurrection the entire way through. Until we understand the function of a passage in light of the general argument of the book it occurs, we are not fully respecting the way God inspired it.

If God inspired each Scripture—meaning at least each "writing" or book of the Bible—to be profitable, we must grapple with each book of the Bible as a whole to fully understand it. (In some cases, where independent units of thought have simply been placed together in a book randomly--for instance, psalms in the Book of Psalms, most proverbs in the Book of Proverbs, and many laws in the legal sections of Exodus and Deuteronomy--this principle is less important. But it is very important as a principle for reading most of Scripture, and especially for tight-knit arguments like Romans or books of interdependent symbols like Revelation.)

This principle has serious implications for our Bible study. Instead of reading verses in the Bible first of all with a concordance or chain-references in our Bible, we need to learn to read books of the Bible straight through. Preferably we should read the smaller books like Mark in one setting; at least we should focus on a particular book for a particular period of time. Merely skipping from book to book without returning to a particular book is unhelpful.

Objections to Context

I should deal here with one objection to context that arises in some circles. Some people quote Scripture out of context and then claim they are right because they have special authority or a special revelation from God. But they should be honest in claiming that this is a special revelation rather than the Scripture. All revelations must be judged (1 Cor 14:29; 1 Thess 5:20-21), and God gave us a Bible in part so we could test other revelations. No one has the right to short-circuit hearers' rights to evaluate their claims from Scripture by claiming a revelation about Scripture's meaning which the hearers cannot evaluate by studying it for themselves. Otherwise anyone could claim that Scripture means anything! Any view can be supported based on proof-texts out of context; any theology can make its reasoning sound consistent; Jehovah's Witnesses do this all the time. We dare not base our faith on other people's study of the Bible rather than on the Bible itself.

We should be very careful what we claim the Bible teaches. Claiming that "The Bible says" is equivalent to claiming, "This is what the Lord says." In Jeremiah's day, some false prophets falsely claimed to be speaking what God was saying, but they were in fact speaking from their own imaginations (Jer 23:16) and stealing their messages from each other (Jer 23:30) rather than listening to God's voice for themselves (Jer 23:22). God can sovereignly speak to people through Scripture out of context if he wishes, just as he can speak through a bird or a poem or a donkey; if God is all-powerful (Rev 1:8), He can speak however He pleases. But we do not routinely appeal to donkeys to teach us truth, and how he speaks to one person through a verse out of context does not determine its meaning for all hearers for all time. The universal meaning of the text is the meaning to which all readers have access, namely, what it means in context.

When I was a young Christian recently converted, I was taking a class in Latin and supposed to be translating Caesar for my homework. Wanting to read only my Bible and not do my homework, I flipped open the Bible and stuck my finger down, hoping to find a text that said, "Forsake all and follow me." Instead, I found, "Render therefore to Caesar the things that are Caesar's, and to God the things that are God's" (Lk 20:25). God chose to answer my foolish approach to Scripture on the level it deserved, but this hardly means that this text now summons all Christians to translate Caesar's *Gallic War*!

All claims to hear God's voice must be evaluated (1 Cor 14:29; 1 Thess 5:20-21), and listening to someone else's claim can get us in trouble if we do not test it carefully (1 Kgs 13:18-22). Paul warns us: "If anyone thinks himself a prophet or spiritual, let him acknowledge that what I write is the Lord's command.

If one ignores this, he himself will be ignored" (1 Cor. 14:37-38). The one revelation to which *all* Christians can look with assurance is the Bible; what we can be sure it means is what God meant when he inspired the original authors to communicate their original message. This is the one revelation all Christians agree on as the "canon," or measuring-stick, for all other claims to revelation. Thus we need to do our best to properly understand it, preach it and teach it the way God gave it to us, in context.

Some claim that the apostles took Scripture out of context in the New Testament, which authorizes us to do the same; some nonbelieving Jewish critics use the same argument to claim that the New Testament writers were not truly inspired by the Holy Spirit. We could respond that, no matter how led by the Spirit we may be, we are not writing Scripture. But the fact is that claims about New Testament writers taking the Old Testament out of context are mostly overrated. The examples critics give usually fall into one of three categories, none of which authorize us to discover a text's meaning by ignoring its context. First, when responding to opponents who used proof-texts, the biblical writers sometimes responded accordingly ("answering a fool according to his folly," as Proverbs says). Second, and much more often, they simply drew analogies from the Old Testament, using them to illustrate a principle found in those texts or the lives they present.

Third, and perhaps most often, the texts we think are out-of-context reflect our own failure to recognize the complex way the writer has used the context. Some non-Christian scholars have accused Matthew of quoting Hosea 11:1 ("Out of Egypt have I called my son") out of context; they often present this as the one of the most blatant cases of the New Testament writers misunderstanding context. They make this claim because Hosea is talking about God delivering Israel from Egypt, whereas Matthew applies the text to Jesus. But Matthew knows the verse quite well: instead of depending on the standard Greek translation of Hosea here, he even makes his own more correct translation from the Hebrew. If we read Matthew's context, we see that this is not the only place where he compares Jesus with Israel: as Israel was tested in the wilderness for forty years, Jesus was tested there forty days (Matt 4:1-2). Matthew also knows Hosea's context: as God once called Israel from Egypt (Hosea 11:1), he would bring about a new exodus and salvation for his people (Hosea 11:10-11). Jesus is the harbinger, the pioneer, of this new era of salvation for his people.

In the same context, Matthew applies Jeremiah 31:15 (where Rachel weeps over Israel's exile) to the slaughter of infants in Bethlehem (Matt 2:17-18), near which Rachel was buried (Gen 35:19). But Matthew knows Jeremiah's context: after announcing Israel's tragedy, God promises restoration (Jer 31:16-17) and a new covenant (Jer 31:31-34). Matthew compares this tragedy in Jesus' childhood to one in Israel's history because he expects his first, biblically knowledgeable readers to recognize that such tragedy formed the prelude to messianic salvation. Matthew also knows very well the context of Isaiah 7:14, which he quotes in Matthew 1:23 (see discussion in chapter 2, below); the context remains fresh in Matthew's mind when he quotes Isaiah 9:1-2 in Matthew 4:15-16. Matthew is not ignoring context: he is comparing Jesus' ministry with Israel's history and the promises those very contexts evoke. He read the context better than his critics have!

Standing before God

In different parts of the body of Christ we teach many different things; our only basis for dialogue is our common foundation in Scripture. But if we can make Scripture say whatever we want by taking it out of context, we will not be able to truly call each other back to a common foundation.

Often interpretation makes a life-and-death difference: for example, in the past some people justified indulgences (paying money to the church to achieve forgiveness) or slavery. This study is about interpretation methods, not doctrines, but let us take for example some views commonly believed today. I am not asking whether we are right or wrong in such teachings, but what the consequences could be if we are wrong. If my teaching (and not just the hearers' misinterpretation) leads people to believe that once they have prayed a prayer they will be saved no matter how they live or what religion they later convert to, I had better be right, or I will have much to answer for before God if I am wrong. Conversely, if my teaching (and not just the hearers' misinterpretation) leads people to be so insecure about their relationship with God that some of them give up in despair, I will have much to answer for before God if I am wrong. If I teach about healing in such a way that people are afraid to trust God, and people suffer or die who could have been restored, I must stand before God. If I teach that everyone with faith will be healed, and if some who are not healed then lose faith, I must stand before God.

The question is not whether we will stand before God, since we will stand before Him no matter what, but whether He will find us faithful or unfaithful to what He has taught us. What we teach can have life-and-death consequences in people's lives. If what we teach is what the Bible really says, the responsibility lies with the Bible and the God who gave it; if what we teach is our misinterpretation of the Bible, we bear the responsibility before God. I can imagine that on the day of judgment many people will protest, "But I was just preaching what so-and-so was preaching." But many "mega-preachers" have spent more time marketing themselves and getting "big" than they have spent researching the Bible. (If you immerse yourself in the Bible, you will be able to tell which is which.) When we stand before God, we cannot blame the mega-preachers for what we have taught. God gave us a Bible not so we could memorize other preachers' proof-texts, but so we could find out what God really teaches us.

In the following chapter, we will survey examples of verses in context—partly to illustrate how desperately we need to study context more carefully, despite the fact that all of us profess to believe in it. I deliberately picked texts that are often taken out of context in the kinds of church circles I know best. I teach students from many denominations (and non-denominations), and find that most of these texts are familiar to the majority of students in their out-of-context form. After examining the texts together in context, however (or allowing the students to study them in context on their own), we usually come to near-unanimous (usually unanimous) consensus on what they mean.

After examining "immediate context" in the next chapter, we will move to other themes in the following chapters. First, we will turn to whole-book context includes learning to recognize the structure of argument (in books with tight-knit arguments like Romans) and developing themes (in books more like Mark). Then we will turn to issues like the situational or historical context—"background"—making sure that we address the same kinds of issues the biblical authors were addressing. We will also turn to the different kinds of writing in the Bible (styles, genres, and forms like parables).

Chapter 2
Learning Context

Although everyone recognizes the importance of context in theory, most Bible readers selectively ignore it in practice. You may be an exception, but do not be too disturbed if you are one of those readers unfamiliar with the actual context of many of the passages we treat in this chapter. I have offered these passages as samples purposely because I have often heard them taken out of context, and my students are frequently surprised when they actually read them in context. Although we may think we read the Bible in context, too often we read the Bible in light of how we have heard others use those same Scripture texts. Whether those interpretations are new or old, they cannot take priority over what the text itself says in context.

You need not agree with our interpretation of every example cited below, but it is important to think through them and to make sure that your view of the text is based on its context rather than how you have heard it used. These examples should illustrate how context makes a difference in our understanding. In no instance are we challenging specific doctrines people have sometimes based on these verses; we are challenging methods of interpretation. (If some texts in context do not support a doctrine, the doctrine might still be defended if other texts support it.) You will learn context principles best if you actually work through the passages yourself before reading our interpretation of them; this way you will recognize what students in my classrooms usually recognize: when most the students come to the same conclusions independently, they recognize for themselves how clear the point of the text is.

We begin with some brief examples of context within verses, but the emphasis of this chapter will be on broader levels of context.

Context *within* Verses

Sometimes readers ignore context even within a single verse. Traditional English poetry balances sounds with rhymes, but ancient Hebrew poetry balanced ideas instead. Most translations place the poetry of Psalms and most of the biblical Prophets in verse form. (The King James Version did not do so, but only because translators in 1611 had not yet rediscovered the idea-balancing pattern.) There are different kinds of idea-balancing, or parallelism, in texts; we mention here only two of the most common.

In one kind of parallelism, the second line repeats the basic idea of the first (sometimes adding or replacing some details)--for instance, "Happy is the one who does not walk in the counsel of the wicked, nor stand in the path traversed by sinners, nor sit in the seat of scoffers" (Ps 1:1). (One would not want to preach three points in a sermon based on these three lines; rather, they are three illustrations of a single point.) In another kind of parallelism, the second line is an explicit contrast with the first; for instance, "Ill-gotten gains do not profit, But righteousness delivers from death" (Prov 10:2, NASB).

In the U.S., many Christians use the line, "Where there is no vision, the people perish" (Prov 29:18), to talk about making a plan. But what does Proverbs mean by "vision"? Does it just mean having a good plan for the future? Does it mean that a driver who needs glasses might run over someone if she drives without her glasses? Because most of the Book of Proverbs is a collection of general principles rather than a sustained argument, the verses around Proverbs 29:18 do not help us interpret the verse very well. The other half of the verse, however, does provide some context. "Where there is no vision, the people perish; but happy is the person who obeys God's law" (Prov. 29:18). The second half of the verse parallels the basic idea of the first half: visions and the law are both sources of God's revelation, sources of hearing from God. In other words, "vision" does not refer to mere natural sight; nor does it merely refer to having a plan for the future; it refers to hearing from God. The Hebrew term translated "vision" here in fact relates to dreams, revelations, or oracles, which confirms the point: God's people needed the Bible and genuine prophets who had heard from God to guide them in the right way.

Proverbs 11:1 warns that God hates a "false balance." Unfortunately, some people today quote this verse to imply that God wants us to be "balanced" people, not too committed to a particular agenda. The real point of the proverb, however, is to avoid cheating our neighbor: the rest of the verse reads, "but God delights in a correct weight." In the markets of ancient Israel, people would weigh out grain or other items in return for a particular weight of money, but some people cheated their customers by changing the scales. The point is: God hates injustice; he hates people cheating their neighbors. This kind of parallelism is frequent in Israelite poetry (for instance, Mary means basically the same thing when she says that her soul "exalts" the Lord as when she declares that her spirit rejoices in God--Lk 1:46-47.)

Another example of within-verse context may be Hosea 4:6: "My people are destroyed for lack of knowledge." Often we get the meaning of this verse correct even without knowing the context, but this may be more because we value the Bible like Hosea did than because the line we quote is explicit by itself.

After all, we could be destroyed for lack of knowledge about driving, test-taking, foreign policy, crime prevention, disease, and so forth. The "knowledge" in this particular verse, however, does not mean all kinds of knowledge. The verse specifically refers to Israel's rejection of God's Law: "...Since you forgot my law" (Hosea 4:6). In other words, God's people are destroyed because they have not paid attention to His Word; they do not know Him because they do not know it.

Helpful as it is to examine the context within a particular verse, in most cases we need a broader circle of context than simply within a verse.

Paragraph Context: Train Yourself

Paragraph context is usually what people mean when they talk about "reading in context." We cannot stop with paragraph context--a work may make a point in a sentence that functions as part of a larger argument within a paragraph, which in turn functions as part of a larger argument within an entire book of the Bible. Nevertheless, context on the level of paragraphs--the immediately related material around a particular verse--is essential to putting verses in context. If you sit in a church service where someone rattles off verse after verse, you need to be able to check each of those verses in context. In time you may learn the Bible well enough that you immediately know the context as soon as anyone quotes a verse; until then, you need to look the verses up and find the context. For your own Bible study, however, do not even begin with isolated verses; read paragraphs (and preferably books) as a whole. Then you will learn these texts right to begin with, namely, in their context.

Instead of simply reading through the rest of this chapter at this point, I highly recommend that you look up the following verses in context and decide for yourself what they mean. Ask yourself the questions we have attached to each of these texts. After you have finished, you may check your own conclusions with our observations on these and other texts below. If our observations bring issues to your attention that you had not considered, you may want to consider them and reread the text (although in the end you are not obligated to accept all our conclusions). If our observations merely confirm your own reading, you can surmise that your context-reading skills are fairly well-developed. The goal is not simply to hold particular views on the sample texts listed below, but to learn the skill of reading *all* Scripture in context. (As a young Christian I used most of the following verses out of context until I began systematically studying the Bible book by book, at which time their context gradually became obvious to me.)

Some of the more difficult passages (toward the end of our list) are more debatable in sense than some of the more obvious ones (toward the beginning). Also, in some cases the passages may include a principle that applies to the point for which people often quote them. But the exercise here is to determine what the text specifically means, so that we can apply the principle in all the appropriate ways and not just in the ways we have often heard.

1. John 10:10: Who is the thief? (Start back at least at 10:1 or 10:5)

2. When Jesus says, "If I am lifted up, I will draw all people to myself" (John 12:32), what does He mean by being "lifted up"?

3. Which day is the "day that the Lord has made" (Ps. 118:24)? Does the text refer to every day (the way most people apply it) or to a specific day? (See Ps. 118:22-23; more generally 118:15-29)

4. Is God's announcement that He owns "the cattle on a thousand hills" (Ps. 50:10) an assurance that He can supply all our needs? Or does it mean something else in context? (Keep in mind that other passages do teach that God supplies our needs; the question here is not whether God will provide, but whether that is what this passage means.)

5. What does the "baptism of fire" refer to in Matt. 3:11? Is it just a purification or empowerment for believers or something else? (Keep in mind that "fire" symbolizes different things in different

passages. The question is, what does "fire" mean in *this* immediate context?)

6. By calling us to "imitate" God (Eph 5:1; King James' "followers" here is literally "imitators"), does Paul want us to speak planets into existence? To be everywhere at once? Check the context (4:32-5:2).

7. What does it mean to resist the devil in James 4:7? In 1 Peter 5:8? In Ephesians 4:27? Some people use these verses to support rebuking the devil whenever something goes wrong. Is that the point?

8. Some people quote Joel 2:9 to say that we are God's mighty army (in a spiritual sense). Other texts may say that, but is that the point of this text?

9. Some people quote Joel 3:10 to say that we should claim God's strength when we are weak. While that is a biblical principle (2 Cor 12:10), is it the point here?

10. More controversially, read Isaiah 14:12-14 in view of the whole of Isaiah 14. To whom does this text refer? (Keep in mind that "Lucifer," found only in the King James Version, is simply a Latin title for the "morning star," not actually found in the Hebrew. Because some interpreters believed this text referred to Satan, they applied the title to Satan, but the Bible does not use the term

anywhere else, so whether or not it is actually Satan's title depends on the meaning of this passage.)

11. Many people apply Ezek 28:12-14 to the devil, just as they apply Is 14 to him. In context, is that really the point of this passage? (Again, we are not questioning whether the devil exists or whether the devil fell. The question is whether *this* passage discusses it.)

12. When Paul says, "I can do all things through Christ who strengthens me" (Phil. 4:13), does he have anything in particular in mind? (I.e., does "all things" mean that he can currently fly, walk through walls, spit fire, and so forth, or does it mean something more specific?)

13. What is the "word of God" (or, "word of Christ" in most translations) in Romans 10:17? Does it specifically refer to the Bible in this case or to something else?

14. 1 Corinthians 13:8-10. Some people quote this passage to claim that spiritual gifts have passed away. But according to the context, when will the gifts of the Spirit pass away? For that matter, what is the function of this chapter in the context of the whole letter to the Corinthians (cf. 12:31; 14:1). What is the function of 13:4-6 in the context of the whole letter to the Corinthians? (You may save

this question until our study on book-context if you wish.)

15. Some people emphasize "now-faith" in Hebrews 11:1, as if faith must be directed toward what we receive in the present. In context, is the sort of faith that Hebrews 11:1 talks about oriented toward receiving something in the present or toward receiving it in the future? (Start back around 10:25 and read through 12:4.)

16. Revelation 3:20. When Jesus knocks at the door, is he trying to get someone converted? (To whom is the verse addressed?)

17. One could say that when God "gave" his Son (Jn 3:16), this refers to giving Jesus at his birth in Bethlehem or giving him to the world when God raised him from the dead. What does "giving" him mean in context?

18. When one seeks first the kingdom, *what* things are added to one (Matt 6:33)?

19. Who are Christ's ambassadors in 2 Corinthians 5:20? Whom are they entreating to be reconciled to God?

20. Some people say that the "witnesses" in Hebrews 12:1 are the dead watching us from heaven. But in the context of Hebrews chapter 11, does "witnesses" refer to those who watch us or to those who testified to the truth of God's claims?

(This one may be harder to see depending on your translation, since some translations do not show the connection of related words in this context.)

21. Some people claim the promise that no weapon formed against them would prosper (Isaiah 54:17). Is this a guarantee for every individual Christian in every circumstance or for God's people as a whole protected by His plan for them?

22. Does Proverbs 23:7 mean that whatever we think about ourselves will come true? ("As a person thinks in their heart, so they are.") Or does it mean something else? (Read 23:6-8.)

23. Does Psalm 18:7-15 refer to Jesus' second coming? Read 18:4-6, 16-19.

24. Who is the rose of Sharon, the lily of the valley, in Song of Solomon 2:1-2?

25. In Matthew 18:18, what does Jesus mean by "binding and loosing"? Does He refer to how to treat demons here, or does He refer to something else? (Read especially 18:15-20.)

26. What is the "coming" to which Jesus refers in John 14:1-3? Does He refer here to His second coming or to something else? (Read 14:4-23, and perhaps 13:36-38.)

27. This final question may be the most difficult one. Read Isaiah 7:14 in context (especially 7:10-16; 8:1-4). In the immediate context, to whom does this newborn son refer? (If your conclusions may disturb you, don't worry; we will clarify them below. But it is important for you to grapple with the text intelligently in its context first, and not simply to interpret the passage according to how you've seen it used elsewhere.)

Paragraph Context: Checking yourself

1. The Thief in John 10:10

Many people assume that the thief in John 10:10 is the devil, but they assume this because they have heard this view many times, not because they examined the text carefully in context. Of course, the devil does come to steal, to kill, and to destroy; but we often quote the verse this way and miss the text's direct applications because we have not stopped to read the verse in context.

When Jesus speaks of "the thief," he speaks from a larger context of thieves, robbers, wolves, and strangers who come to harm the sheep (10:1, 5, 8, 10, 12). In this context, those who came before Jesus, claiming his authority, were thieves and robbers (10:8); these tried to approach the sheep without going through the shepherd (10:1). This was because they wanted to exploit the sheep, whereas Jesus was prepared to die defending his sheep from these thieves, robbers, and wolves.

The point becomes even clearer if we start further back in the context. In chapter 9, Jesus heals a blind man and the religious officials kick the blind man out of the religious community for following Jesus. Jesus stands up for the formerly blind man and calls the religious leaders spiritually blind (9:35-41). Because there were no chapter breaks in the original Bible, Jesus' words that continue into chapter 10 are still addressed to the religious leaders. He declares that He is the true Shepherd and the true sheep follow His voice, not the voice of strangers (10:1-5). Those who came before Him were thieves and robbers, but Jesus was the sheep's true salvation (10:8-9). The thief comes only to destroy, but Jesus came to give life (10:10).

In other words, the thief represents the false religious leaders, like the Pharisees who kicked the healed man out of their synagogue. The background of the text clarifies this point further. In Jeremiah 23 and Ezekiel 34, God was the shepherd of His scattered people, His sheep; these Old Testament passages also speak of false religious leaders who abused their authority over the sheep like many of the religious leaders of Jesus' day and not a few religious leaders in our own day.

2. Jesus' Crucifixion in John 12:32

In my country, Christians often sing, "Lift Jesus higher...He said, 'If I be lifted up from the earth, I will draw all men unto Me,'" based on John 12:32. The Bible does talk about "exalting" God and "lifting him up" in praise, but that is not the point of this text. If one reads the next verse (which explicitly says that Jesus was referring to his death), it is clear that "lifting him up" refers to his death on the cross. (The play on words with "lifting up" was already used in both Greek and Hebrew for forms of hanging, such as crucifixion.) Thus, if the song means by lifting Him up what the biblical verse means, we would be singing, "Crucify Him! Crucify Him!" Of course God knows our hearts, but one wonders why a song writer would base a song, which millions of people might sing, on a verse yet not take the time to look up the verse on which it is based!

John three times refers to Jesus being "lifted up": in one case, he compares this event to the serpent being lifted up in the wilderness (Jn 3:14), to make eternal life available to everyone (3:15). In the second, Jesus declares that His adversaries will lift Him up (8:28). In other words, John means by "lifting up" what Isaiah meant by it: Jesus would be crucified (Isa. 52:13 with Isa. 52:14-53:12). John includes plays on words in his gospel, and may also indicate that we "exalt" Jesus by preaching the Cross; but leaves no doubt as to the primary sense of the term in this context: crucifixion.

To read it any other way is to ignore his explicit, inspired explanation of the "lifting up."

3. The Day of Christ's Exaltation in Psalm 118:24

Many churches sing or open services by quoting, "This is the day that the Lord has made." When we sing this, most of us mean that God has made every day and what comes with it, and that we should therefore rejoice in what happens on that day. This is a true principle, but we would do better to quote a different text to prove it (maybe Eph. 5:20). The text we are quoting or singing (and there is nothing wrong with quoting or singing it) actually offers us a different, dramatic cause for celebration.

In context, Psalm 118:24 refers not to every day, but to a particular, momentous day: the day when the Lord made the rejected stone the cornerstone (118:22-23), probably of the Temple (118:19-20, 27). It speaks of a special day of triumph for the Davidic king, applicable in principle to many of God's great triumphs but usually applied in the New Testament in a special way. If Psalm 118:22-23 was fulfilled in Jesus' ministry as He claimed (Mark 12:10-11), so also was Psalm 118:24: the great and momentous day the Lord had made, the day the Psalmist calls his hearers to celebrate, is the prophetic day when God exalted Jesus, rejected by the chief priests, as the cornerstone of His new temple (cf. Eph. 2:20). The verse points to a truth far more significant than merely the common biblical truth that God is with us daily; it points to the greatest act of God on our behalf, when Jesus our Lord died and rose again for us.

4. Cattle in Psalm 50:10

Some people insist that God can supply all our needs because, after all, He "owns the cattle on a thousand hills" (Ps. 50:10); some go beyond God supplying all our needs to suggest that He will supply anything we want. It is in fact true that God can supply all our needs, but there are other texts that explicitly make that point. Psalm 50:10, by contrast, does not address the issue of God supplying our needs (and certainly not all our wants); rather, it declares that God does not need our sacrifices.

The figurative setting of Psalm 50 is a courtroom, where God has summoned His people to respond to His charges. He summons heaven and earth as His witnesses (50:1-6)--as witnesses of the covenant (see Deut. 32:1; cf. Ps. 50:5), they would be witnesses concerning Israel's violation of that covenant. Israel has some reason to be nervous; God is not only the offended party in the case, but the Judge (Ps. 50:4, 6), not to mention the accusing witness! Testifying against them, God declares, "I am your God" (50:7)--reminding them of the covenant He had made with them. They had not broken faith against Him by failing to offer sacrifices (50:8)—in fact, God has little concern about these sacrifices. "I don't need your animal sacrifices," he declares, "for all the animals belong to Me, including the cattle on a thousand hills. I don't eat animal flesh, but if I did, would I tell you if I were hungry? Since I own these creatures, wouldn't I just take them if I wanted them?" (50:9-13). The sacrifice which He really requires is thanksgiving and obedience (50:14-15; cf. 50:23). But He would prosecute (50:21) the wicked who broke His covenant (50:16-20).

Most ancient near Eastern peoples believed that their gods depended on them for sacrifices, and if their gods were overpowered, their nation would be overpowered as well. The God of Israel reminds them that He is not like the pagan gods around them. Unlike Baal of the Canaanites (whose temples included a bed), Zeus of the Greeks (whom Hera put to sleep so her Greeks could win a battle), and other deities, the God of Israel neither slumbered nor slept (Ps. 121:3-4). God does not mention the cattle on a thousand hills to promise us anything we want (as a song pointed out some years ago, many of us don't need any cows at the moment anyway); He mentions the cattle to remind us that He is not dependent on us, and we are not doing Him a favor by serving Him.

5. Baptized with Fire in Matthew 3:11

One modern denomination in the U.S. is the "Fire-Baptized Holiness Church"; many other Christians also happily claim to be "baptized in the Holy Ghost and fire." We know and appreciate, of course, what they mean; they mean holiness, and holiness is essential. But is that what John the Baptist means by "fire baptism" in this passage? Fire is sometimes used as a symbol of God's consuming holiness or of purifying trials in the Bible; but when fire is conjoined with the image of baptism in the New Testament, it has to do not with mere purification of the individual, but with purifying the whole world by judgment. (Judgment is the most common symbolic application fire in the Bible.) Rather than cross-referencing to other passages that use the image of fire in different ways, we ought to examine what the "baptized in fire" text means in its own context. We ought to use the passage itself before jumping to a concordance.

The context is a call to repentance, and much of the audience promised this fire baptism was unwilling to repent. John the Baptist was immersing people in water as a sign of their repentance and preparation for the coming Kingdom of God (Matt. 3:2, 6). (Jewish people used baptism when non-Jews would convert to Judaism, but John demanded that even religious Jewish people come to God on the same terms on which Gentiles should; cf. 3:9.) John warned the Pharisees about God's coming wrath (3:7), and that unless they bore fruit (3:8) God's ax of judgment would cast them into the fire (3:10; cf. 12:33). Fruitless trees were worthless except for fuel. But chaff was barely even useful as fuel (it burned quickly), yet the chaff of which John spoke would be burned with "unquenchable"— eternal—"fire" (3:12).

In the verses just before and just after our verse, "fire" is hellfire (3:10, 12). When John the Baptist speaks of a baptism in fire, he uses an image of judgment that follows through the whole paragraph. Remember that John's hearers here are not repentant people (3:7). The Messiah is coming to give his audience a twofold baptism, and different members of his audience would experience different parts of it. Some may repent, be gathered into the barn and receive the Spirit. The unrepentant, however, would be chaff, trees cut down, and would receive the fire!

6. Imitating God in Ephesians 5:1

This passage summons us to imitate God the way children imitate a father. The text is also specific, however, in the ways that we should imitate God: we should forgive as God in Christ forgave us (4:32) and love one another, just as Christ sacrificially loved us (5:2). Happily, the text does not require us to imitate God by being all-powerful or everywhere at once!

7. *Resisting the Devil in James 4:7; 1 Peter 5:8-9; Ephesians 4:27*

James contrasts the peaceful wisdom which is from God (3:13, 17-18; "from above" was a typical Jewish way of saying, "from God") with the contentious wisdom which is from the devil (3:14-15). Then he warns his audience not to try to hold both perspectives as if they were compatible. Those who try to follow both God's and the world's wisdom at the same time are spiritual adulteresses (4:4).

Submitting to God and resisting the devil (4:7), then, is rejecting the world's evil way of treating one another and preferring the gentle approach that comes from God. To adopt this new way of treating others requires repentance (4:8-10).

1 Peter refers to a situation in which Christians are being persecuted (1 Pet 4:12-16); in 1 Peter 5:8-9, the devil apparently seeks to crush believers by seeking to turn them from the faith. Resisting him therefore means withstanding the persecution. In the context of Ephesians 4:27, one resists the devil by refusing to deceive or stay angry with one's fellow-believers (4:25-26); in the whole context of Ephesians, this is part of "spiritual warfare" (6:11-14, 18).

8. God's Locust Army in Joel 2:9

Although the third chapter of Joel seems to describe a future war, chapters one and two depict as an invading army a devastating locust plague (Joel 1:4; 2:25). This text does not depict the church as a spiritual army of evangelists (a truth offered by plenty of other biblical passages); it depicts locusts as an agricultural judgment against the sins of God's people.

9. The Strength of the Weak in Joel 3:10

This passage is not an invitation to the weary righteous to strengthen themselves; nor is it talking about God's power perfected in our weakness (central as that biblical message is). God is speaking in judgment to the nations gathered against his people for the final war (Joel 3:9). God mockingly invites the enemies of his people to gather against him, make their weapons and make themselves strong, when in fact they are hopelessly weak before them. Then he promises to destroy them! He is actually mocking the enemies of his people as he invites them to judgment (3:12-14).

10. Babylon's Ruler in Isaiah 14

The full context of this passage would let us know that Isaiah is denouncing a ruler, even if he did not tell us so explicitly. Like many other ancient

Israelite prophets, Isaiah includes oracles against various nations: Babylon (Isa. 13-14), Moab (Isa. 15-16), Damascus (Isa. 17), the Nubian and Egyptian empires (Isa. 18-20), Babylon again (21:1-10), Edom (21:11-12), Arabia (21:13-17), Jerusalem (22), and Tyre (23). Isaiah 14:3-4 explicitly tell us that the following oracle is directed against the ruler of Babylon--an oppressor (14:4), a ruler (14:5), who conquered other nations (14:6). As he is defeated, the nations rejoice (14:7); figuratively speaking, even the trees of Lebanon rejoice, for he will no longer be cutting them down for his building projects (14:8). How has the Lord brought this king low, breaking his rod and scepter (14:5)?

The text clearly indicates that he is *dead*: he goes to Sheol, the realm of the dead (14:9), and other rulers there rejoice that the ruler who defeated them has died just like them (14:9-10). His pomp and dignity ruined, his court harpists silenced, he now rots with maggots and worms consuming his flesh (14:11)--i.e., he is a corpse. This description does not fit the devil very well, but it does fit a human ruler who exalted himself hence was brought low for his arrogance.

Like Israel whose glory was cast from heaven to earth (Lam. 2:1), this ruler has been cast from heaven to earth. At this point some readers think that the subject must change to a literal fall from heaven, in which case, they say, it must be applied to a fallen angel like the devil. But the jubilant outcries of Lebanon's cedars in

14:8 was hardly literal; neither was the image of dead rulers rising from their thrones in the realm of the dead in 14:9 (would they still be enthroned)? Hebrew poetry painted pictures with words, just as poetry normally does today; in contrast to non-poetic parts of Isaiah, the poetic portions are consistently full of figurative speech. Other texts also speak of figurative falls from heaven, most of them without applying them to the devil (Amos 9:2; Matt 11:23; Lk 10:15).

Kings of Babylon, like some other ancient near Eastern kings, actually claimed to be gods (compare, for example, Dan 3:5; 6:7). Claiming to be a deity like the morning star or offspring of the sun god or deity of dawn would not be unnatural for an ancient near Eastern ruler, but Isaiah grants the title only in contemptuous mockery: "Poor king of Babylon! You reached for heaven, but have been cast down to earth! You tried to raise yourself above God, but now you have died like a man!" (compare the similar taunt in Ps. 82:6-8). Verses 12-14 refer to the king of Babylon just like the preceding verses do: he once conquered nations (14:12), wanted to be enthroned on the sacred mountain (perhaps referring to Babylon's future conquest of Mount Zion in Jerusalem) (14:13), and he was brought down to Sheol, the realm of the dead (14:15).

The following context drives home the point still more thoroughly: this is "the man" who struck fear into the hearts of nations (14:16), "the man" whose conquests made lands deserted, destroying cities, carrying peoples off into captivity (14:17). Unlike the other nations' kings who at least were buried in dignity in royal tombs (a final honor very important to ancient people's sense of honor), this king's corpse was thrown out in the open to rot, trampled underfoot in punishment for the violent destruction he had brought upon his own people (14:18-20). His descendants and those of his people, Babylon, would be cut off (14:21-22). The text could not be any plainer in context: this explicit oracle against the king of Babylon (14:3-23) would be fulfilled in its time, and God's oppressed people vindicated.

Despite the clarity of this text, some readers remain so committed to their earlier understanding of the text that they are determined to get around the context. "Well, maybe it does refer to the king of Babylon, but it *must* refer to the devil, too," they protest. But why must it refer to the devil? Is there anything here that cannot refer to an earthly ruler exalting himself? Do any of the oracles against other nations (chs. 13-23) contain hidden prophecies against the devil? Was the devil a mere earthly conqueror, brought to the realm of the dead after he was thrust from heaven (14:12, 15)? "But we all know that Lucifer refers to the devil, and that the devil said he would ascend to heaven," one student protested to me. "How do we know it?" I replied. The view that "Lucifer" refers to the devil and that the devil promised to ascend to heaven is based on an interpretation of the King James translation of this text. If "Lucifer" appeared here, it would be the only place in the Bible it occurred, but it does not in fact occur here, either. The Hebrew does not speak of "Lucifer" here; that is a Latin title for the "morning star" which the King James Version used in its translation here. Even if we granted that this text "also" refers to the devil, however, why is it that many readers quote it as applying to the devil but not to what it straightforwardly says, namely, a sinning human? Perhaps if we applied the text more as a warning against human pride, many would not want to preach from it any more than they preach from the surrounding chapters (which is little indeed!)

Unable to make their case in Isaiah 14, some students declare that Isaiah 14 must refer to the devil because Ezekiel 28 does. There are two fallacies in this argument. First of all, Ezekiel 28 and other passages could refer to the fall of the devil without Isaiah 14 having to do with that subject; no one is denying that some texts in the Bible refer to fallen angels, only that this is the point of Isaiah 14. The second fallacy of the argument is that Ezekiel 28 is not one of the texts referring to fallen angels, either.

11. Tyre's Ruler in Ezekiel 28

Like Isaiah, Ezekiel also has oracles against the nations: Ammon (25:1-7), Moab (25:8-11), Edom (25:12-14), Philistia (25:15-17), Tyre (26:1-28:19), Sidon (28:20-26), and Egypt (29:1-32:32). The passage sometimes applied to the devil, 28:12b-19, is in the heart of an oracle against the ruler of Tyre; in fact, verse 12 begins, "Son of man, take up this lament against the ruler of Tyre." No one disputes that the context refers to the ruler of Tyre, but those who apply the text to the devil declare that it also applies to him, because (they claim) some features of the text cannot apply to anyone but the devil.

This argument, as we shall see, is not actually accurate. The lament calls this ruler arrogant about his wisdom and perfection of beauty (28:12, 17)--just as Tyre claimed to be perfect in beauty (27:3-4, 11) and full of wisdom that brought wealth (28:3-4), self-proclaimed wisdom that made the ruler think he was a god (28:6) though he was but a human being (28:8-10). This ruler was in Eden, the garden of God (28:13), which advocates of the devil-interpretation think must be taken literally: only the devil was in Eden, they say. But this claim is not true; Adam and Eve, who did seek equality with God (Gen. 3:5), also lived in Eden, and Ezekiel could compare the Tyrian ruler's hubris with that of the first people.

Yet another explanation is better than either the devil-interpretation or the Adam-interpretation: Ezekiel explicitly compares the ruler of Babylon to a cherub (28:14-15). Genesis calls neither Adam nor the serpent a cherub, but does refer explicitly to cherubim in the garden: God's angels stationed there to keep Adam and Eve out after their fall (Gen. 3:24; cf. Ezek. 28:14-15 NIV: "guardian cherub"). In other words, this is an image representing great prestige in God's garden. (The "holy mountain of God"--28:14--might allude to Mount Zion, as often in Scripture, in which case the image of cherubim probably also recalls the cherubim on which God was enthroned on the ark in the Temple. The blamelessness until found wicked-- 28:15--may also be part of the cherub image.)

Some have objected that the king cannot simply be *compared* to a glorious cherub in Eden; the text calls him a cherub, and must be interpreted literally. Those who insist that all details of such prophecies should be taken literally, however, are not consistent in how they interpret other references to Eden in surrounding chapters. Ezekiel himself is full of graphic, poetic images and metaphors (comparisons in which one thing is simply called another without "like" or "as"), one of which is a statement that Pharaoh was a tree in Eden, God's garden (Ezek. 31:1-18; he is also a sea monster, 29:3-5). Drawing on various images from the account of Adam and Eve's fall, Ezekiel's prophecies speak both of the stately cherubim and the greatest trees in Eden (perhaps the tree of life or the tree of the knowledge of good and evil?) Perhaps advocates of the devil-interpretation press their case that being in Eden refers to the devil in Ezekiel 28 but not in Ezekiel 31 because they can only fit Ezekiel 28 into their view in some other respects. (Some cite the "pipes" on his body, but this is based on only one translation, which the Hebrew does not appear to support here.)

The adornment of precious stones (28:13) alludes to Tyre's great wealth, elsewhere described in terms of gorgeous array (27:4-7, 24) and trade in diverse merchandise including precious stones (27:16, 22). The wickedness of 28:15 is the wickedness of Tyre's merchant interests (28:16), her "dishonest trade" (28:18 NIV) elsewhere referred to in the context (27:2-36; 28:4-5; cf. 26:17). The king's pride on account of his beauty (28:17) recalls the pride of the ruler of Tyre who claims to be a god yet is merely a man (28:2), proud because of the wealth Tyre had amassed through trading (28:5). That fire would come forth from the ruler of Tyre (28:18), just as ancient cities were normally destroyed by burning in their midst (cf. e.g., Amos 1:4, 7, 12; 2:2, 5--especially Amos 1:10, against Tyre).

Ezekiel refers to an arrogant human ruler. The ruler in this passage exalts himself in pride and is cast down; the casting down is more explicit in the oracle earlier in the chapter (28:2-10). He claimed to be a god, enthroned in the heart of the seas (28:2; Tyre was off the seacoast of Phoenicia). God has Ezekiel mock this ruler: You think that you are as wise as a god (28:6), but God would bring judgment on this ruler by other nations (28:7); then would he still pretend to be a god in front of those who would kill him (28:9)? He was a "man," not a god, and he would die a horrible and violent death (28:8-10). This is hardly a description of the devil, an immortal spirit; this is an earthly ruler who claimed to be a god, who would learn his mortality at the time of God's judgment on Tyre.

Yet even if these two passages referred to the devil as well as to earthly rulers—though in context they do not—why do defenders of this view often apply these passages to the devil yet never apply them also to earthly rulers judged by God for their arrogance? Wouldn't examples of human arrogance make even more useful passages for preaching or teaching matters relevant to our hearers? I suspect that many believers simply assume these passages refer to the devil because that is the way we have always heard them interpreted, but many of us never closely examined them in context. Whatever their views, I do not believe any reader can miss our point: this passage has a broad context in the surrounding chapters, and our short-cuts to learning the Bible have failed to study the books of the Bible the way God inspired them to be written.

12. *Strengthened for Contentment in Philippians 4:13*

A football player at a Christian college approached his Bible professor, greatly troubled. His coach had encouraged the team that they could "do all things through Christ who strengthens" them, citing Philippians 4:13. Yet the team had lost a few games, and the student was unable to fathom why his team was not always winning, since they "could do all things through Christ." The problem, of course, is not with the text, but with the view that the player and apparently his coach had read into the verse. The football player was assuming that Paul had in view matters like winning football games.

Thanking the Philippians for sending him a love-gift (4:10, 14), Paul noted that he had learned contentment with both little and with much (4:12); he could do all things through Christ (4:13). In this context, he is saying that by Christ's strength he could rejoice whether he had much or little. Today we should learn to rejoice in whatever our situation, knowing that Christ strengthens us to endure: whether persecution, ridicule, or even losing a football game.

13. Saving Faith through the Gospel in Romans 10:17

Some people quote Romans 10:17 to support repeating Bible verses to ourselves aloud: "Faith comes by hearing, and hearing by the word of God." Of course, repeating the Bible to ourselves is important (if we understand it in context). But those who think that is the point of this particular *verse* should reexamine the context of Romans 10:17.

Paul argues that no one could be saved unless they heard this word, which is the message of Christ (10:14-15), the "report" of the witnesses (10:16). This is also the "word" in their mouths and hearts through which they are saved (10:8-10). Faith could only come from hearing this word, the gospel of Christ (10:17). In contrast to Hebrews 11:1, where "faith" in context means persevering faith, this passage refers to saving faith. One cannot be saved until one hears the truth about Jesus.

14. 1 Corinthians 13:8-10 in Context

Paul says that spiritual gifts like prophecy, tongues and knowledge will pass away when we no longer need them (1 Cor. 13:8-10). Some Christians read this passage as if it said, "Spiritual gifts like prophecy, tongues, and knowledge passed away when the last book of the New Testament was written." This interpretation of 1 Corinthians 13 ignores the entire context of 1 Corinthians, however: it is a letter to the Corinthians in the middle of the first century, and they had never yet heard of a New Testament in the middle of the first century. Had Paul meant the completion of the New Testament, he would have had to have made this point much more clearly--starting by explaining what a New Testament addition to their Bible was.

In the context we find instead that Paul means that spiritual gifts will pass away when we know God as He knows us, when we see Him face to face (13:12; when we no longer see as through a mirror as in the present—cf. 2 Cor 3:18, the only other place where Paul uses the term). In other words, spiritual gifts must continue until our Lord Jesus returns at the end of the age. They should remain a normal part of our Christian experience today.

A broader examination of the context reveals even more of Paul's meaning in this passage. In chapters 12-14, Paul addresses those who are abusing particular spiritual gifts, and argues that God has gifted all members of Christ's body with gifts for building up God's people. Those who were using God's gifts in ways that hurt others were abusing the gifts God had given for helping others. That is why Paul spends three paragraphs in the midst of his discussion of spiritual gifts on the subject of love: gifts without love are useless (13:1-3); love seeks to edify (13:4-7); the gifts are temporary (for this age only), but love is eternal (13:8-13). We should seek the best gifts (1 Cor. 12:31; 14:1), and love gives us the insight to see which gifts are the best in any given situation--those that build others up.

The context of Paul's entire letter drives this point home further: Paul's description of what love is in 1 Cor. 13:4-7 contrasts starkly with Paul's prior descriptions of the Corinthians in his letter: selfish, boastful, and so on (1 Cor 3:3; 4:6-7, 18; 5:2). The Corinthian Christians, like the later church in Laodicea (Rev. 3:14-22), had a lot in their favor, but lacked what mattered most of all: the humility of love.

15. Persevering Faith in Hebrews 11:1

Hebrews 11:1 declares that "faith is the substance of things hoped for, the evidence of things not seen." Although the verse expresses faith in terms of what we hope for--suggesting a future emphasis--some popular preachers have emphasized the first word of the verse in many translations: "Now." They read "now" as if it were an adjective describing faith: "Hebrews says 'now-faith,' so if it's not 'now,' it's not 'faith.'" Thus, they claim, one must have faith for the answer now; if one merely believes that God eventually *will* answer the prayer, they claim that one does not have faith.

Other passages may stress the importance of believing God in the present (like the woman with the flow of blood touching Jesus' garment), but that is not the point of this passage. First, the English word "now" is not an adjective but an adverb; thus the English text, if it referred to time at all, would not mean, "the now-kind-of-faith is," but "faith *currently* is" (i.e., "now" does not describe faith). But second, the passage was not written in English; it was written in Greek, and the Greek word translated "now" here does not have anything to do with time at all. It simply means "but" or "and"—"And faith is." (It is "now" only as in "Now once upon a time"—this particular Greek word never has to do with time.) The popular preachers apparently were in such a hurry to get their doctrine out that they never bothered to look the verse up in Greek.

Context makes it clear that this verse addresses reward in the future, not the present. The first readers of Hebrews had endured great sufferings (Heb. 10:32-34), but some were no longer pursuing Christ with their whole hearts, and some were in danger of falling away (10:19-31). The writer thus exhorts the readers not to abandon their hope, which God would reward if they persevered (10:35-37); he trusted that they would persevere in faith rather than falling back to destruction (10:38-39). That persevering faith was the faith that laid hold on God's promises for the future, the kind of faith great heroes of faith had exhibited in the past: for instance, we know Enoch had this faith, for the Bible says that he pleased God, and no one can please God without such faith (11:5-6).

Most of Hebrews 11's examples of faith are examples of persevering faith in hope of future reward: Abraham left his present land seeking a city whose builder and maker was God (11:8-10); Joseph looked ahead to the exodus which would happen long after his death (11:22); Moses rejected Egypt's present treasures in favor of future reward (11:24-26); and so on. The writer concludes with those heroes of the faith who suffered and died without deliverance in this life (11:35-38). In fact, though history commended the faith of all the heroes of this chapter, the writer declares that *none* of them received what God had promised them (11:39-40).

Finally the writer points to the ultimate hero of the faith--the author and perfecter of our faith, who endured the cross in hope of his future reward, the joy of His exaltation at God's right hand (12:1-3). If all these men and women of faith had endured in the past, why did the Hebrews balk at the shedding of their blood (12:4), at the trials which were just the Lord's temporary discipline (12:5-13)? Instead of falling away (12:14-29) because of their persecution, they were to stand firm in Christ, not being moved away from the hope of their calling. "Faith" in this context means not a momentary burst of conviction, but a perseverance tested by trials and time that endures in light of God's promises for the future.

16. Knocking at the Door in Revelation 3:20

Here Jesus knocks not at the door of the individual sinner, but rather at the door of a church that was acting like one! Whereas Jesus had set before another church an open door, inviting them into his presence despite the false accusations of their persecutors (Rev 3:8), he was here locked out of another church. Ancient hospitality required sharing food with a guest, but the Laodicean church had locked Jesus out by their arrogant self-sufficiency (3:17-18). He wanted these Christians to repent and express again their need for him (3:19).

This does not make illegitimate the faith of those led to Christ using this verse; the principle applies, and it is in any case the gospel message, not the interpretation of a verse, that converted them. But the point remains that if we misinterpret the verse, we do not learn what *this passage* has to say to us. There may be arrogant churches today that have locked Jesus out.

17. God gave his Son in John 3:16

The context indicates that God gave His Son, in the particular sense in which John 3:16 means it, when Jesus was lifted up (3:14-15). In the context of the rest of the Gospel of John, this must mean that he was "lifted up" on the cross (see 8:28; 12:32-33). God gave His Son when Jesus died for our sins. This is the climactic expression of His love for humanity.

18. Seeking First the Kingdom in Matthew 6:33

Jewish people sometimes used Gentiles--non-Jews, who were usually what they would have regarded as "pagans"—as examples of what upright Jews should avoid. "Pagans" seek food, drink, and clothing, Jesus said, but you should not seek these things (6:31-32). Instead, Jesus' followers should seek his kingdom, and these other things—the basic necessities of life— would be taken care of (6:33). It may be no coincidence that Jesus had just taught his disciples to pray first for the agendas of God's kingdom (6:9-10) and only after that for their own basic needs (6:11-13).

19. Christ's Ambassadors in 2 Corinthians 5:20

In every or almost every instance of "we" in the preceding chapters (and probably even in 5:21 which follows, though that is debated), Paul refers to himself and his ministry colleagues. Probably in 5:20, then, Paul also refers not to all Christians as ambassadors, but only to those who are bringing God's message of reconciliation. After all, those he is entreating to be reconciled to God are the Christians in Corinth, who are not ambassadors but those who need ambassadors to them (6:1-2)!

Perhaps ideally all Christians *should* be bringing God's message of reconciliation, but in practice most of the Christians in Corinth weren't. The Corinthian Christians were *acting* like non-Christians, so Paul and his colleagues act as representatives for Christ's righteousness to them, just as Christ represented our sin for us on the cross (5:21). (Paul may be using hyperbole, a figure of speech that means "rhetorical overstatement to graphically emphasize a point").

20. Witnesses in Hebrews 12:1

In this case not all translations make equally clear the terms in the context related to the term for "witnesses" in 12:1. The concept, however, is evident in at least some of them. In the preceding context, God frequently "testified as a witness" or provided "testimony as a witness" that his servants had proved faithful (11:2, 4-5, 39). It is therefore possible that he speaks of the righteous listed in Hebrews 11 as those who also testified what they knew about God. These may be not "witnesses" like those who watch a sports match in a stadium, but rather those who "witness" for or "testify" about the truth they have discovered about God.

21. God's Vindication in Isaiah 54:17

The context indicates that the passage focuses on God's people. Israel had sinned, been judged, but now would be restored, and those who had tried to oppose Israel would be crushed. There is a principle here that God vindicates his people; but it is not an ironclad guarantee for every circumstance in the short run for each individual (though he often does provide protection for Christians, he does not do so all the time; many Christians have died as faithful martyrs). It does encourage us, however, that God will ultimately vindicate his servants and his plans for history. So whatever we must face in the short run, in the long run we can be sure of God's faithfulness and vindication if we remain faithful to him.

22. The Real Heart of a Host in Proverbs 23:7

In the ancient Mediterranean world, sharing food obligated people to loyalty to one another. But Proverbs warns that you cannot trust your host if he is selfish; he may encourage you to eat as much as you like, but you will be sorry if you trust him. What matters is not what he says to you, but what he really thinks in his heart (23:6-8).

23. The Psalmist's Deliverance in Psalm 18:7-15

The language of Psalm 18:7-15 sounds like a cosmic event that shakes all of creation. But ancient Israelite songs, like some of our songs today, could express praise poetically. In this case, the psalmist describes a time when God delivered him personally (18:4-6, 16-

70

19). The deliverance sounds like it affects all creation, but in fact it reflects the dramatic experience of the psalmist, from whose perspective God's intervention seemed too dramatic to narrate in any less cosmic manner.

24. Married Love in Song of Solomon 2:1-2

Many Christian songs depict Jesus as the "lily of the valley," the "rose of Sharon," and the "fairest of ten thousand." The songs are beautiful, and their point is that Jesus is the greatest beauty and desire of our souls. We should not read the meaning of those beautiful songs back onto the meaning of the Song of Solomon, however; the "rose of Sharon" in this book does not refer to Jesus, directly or indirectly. This book is an ancient love song, which provides wonderful insights into romance, the language of marital desire and appreciation, dealing with conflicts in marriage (the brief conflict is 5:2-6), the power of jealousy (8:6), etc. To the extent that it reflects the beauty of marital love, it may also supply us with words in our passionate pursuit of Christ, but this is not the direct subject of the book; the book is a practical example of romantic, married love. (For instance, the "banquet house" and "banner" in 2:4 may refer to ancient wedding customs: while guests were banqueting at the wedding feast, bride and groom consummated their marriage and reportedly hung out a banner when they had sealed their union sexually. It is doubtful that we should read such details as a symbol of Christ; it reads much better as a picture of married sexual love in ancient Israel.)

But even if Song of Solomon were but a symbol of Christ and His Church, as some have supposed, "rose of Sharon" and "lily of the valley" could not refer to Christ. As in the NIV, it is the bride who declares, "I am a rose of Sharon, a lily of the valley"—i.e., as beautiful as the most beautiful of flowers; her groom had made her feel loved, despite her own insecurities (1:6). The groom also compares her to a lily (2:2; 7:2); she compares his approach to one who moves among the lilies (2:16; 6:2-3; he also applies this image to her in 4:5). Even if Song of Solomon were an allegory of Christ and the Church (which is very unlikely), "rose of Sharon" would not refer to Christ, but to His Church. More likely, it is an example of the beautiful romantic language that an inspired author could apply to his bride, as an inspired guide emphasizing the importance of romantic affection in our marriages today.

25. Church Discipline in Matthew 18:18

I used to follow a popular misinterpretation of this verse. As a young Christian, I used to use Matthew 18:18 to "bind" and "loose" demons whenever I would pray (as if demons were always standing by listening). Fortunately, God is more concerned with our faith than with our formulas, and graciously answered my prayers whether or not I threw any "binding" in. But one day I read Matthew 18:18 in context, and I realized that I had been misinterpreting the passage. Because my prayers had "worked," I decided to keep "binding" and "loosing"—but now that I knew better, the practice did not work anymore, because I could no longer do it in the integrity of my heart before God! Happily, I found that God still answered my prayers prayed in Jesus' name without "binding."

What do "binding" and "loosing" mean in this context? In the context, Jesus indicates that if one's fellow-Christian is living a sinful lifestyle, one must confront that Christian; if he or she refuses to listen, one should bring others so one will have two or three witnesses if one must bring the matter before the church. If despite repeated loving confrontations that person refuses to repent, the church must put that person out of the church to teach the person repentance (Matt. 18:15-17). In this context, Jesus declares that whatever they "bind" or "loose" on earth will have already been "bound" or "loosed" in heaven--i.e., under these circumstances, they clearly act on God's authority (18:18). Because the terms "binding" and "loosing" literally have to do with imprisoning or releasing people, and Jewish teachers used these terms to describe their legal authority, the terms make good sense in this context: the church must discipline its erring members, removing them from participation in the church if they continue in unapologetic sin.

The "two or three" who pray in this context (18:19) refer to the two or three witnesses (18:16). I used to read this passage and worry that my prayers would be less efficacious if I could not find someone to join me in prayer; I did wonder, however, why my own faith would be insufficient. But this verse does not imply that prayer is efficacious only for a minimum of two persons; it promises that even if only two witnesses are available, and even if the prayers or actions on earth involve something as serious as withdrawing a person from the church, God will back up His servants whom He has authorized.

Perhaps the specific prayer in mind is a prayer that God will bring the disfellowshiped person to repentance and restoration; if so, Jesus deliberately contrasts the attitude required of His followers with the two or three witnesses in the Old Testament law, who were to be the first to stone those against whom they testified (Deut. 17:7). Probably alluding to a Jewish saying circulating in the early centuries of this era—"Wherever two or three gather to study God's law, His presence is among them"—Jesus assures His followers (specifically the witnesses) of His presence even in the difficult situation of church discipline (Matt 18:20). Of course the principle of answered prayer applies to other prayers as well, but he specifies "two or three" here because he is referring to the "two or three" he just mentioned.

Although we cannot take space here to comment further on the matter, this particular passage does not support the common practice of "binding" demons as it is done today. Whereas "binding demons" in the way it is generally practiced today has no warrant in this text, however, it does appear in some ancient magical texts, which makes this practice even more suspect. When Jesus claims to have "bound the strong man" (Matt 12:29), he does not first tell Satan, "I bind you" before casting out demons. He had already defeated the strong man by overcoming temptation and obeying the Father's will; thus He was free to exercise His authority and cast out demons.

26. Jesus' Post-resurrection Coming in John 14:3

Jesus tells His disciples, "In my Father's house are many 'dwelling-places'" (14:2; "mansions" comes from the Latin translation--it is not in the original Greek text). Jesus promises that He is going to prepare a place for His disciples, but will return and take them to be with Him where He is (John 14:2-3). Usually readers today assume that Jesus here refers to his future coming to take us to heaven or the new earth. If we had these verses by themselves, that view would make as much sense as any other; after all, Jesus often spoke of His second coming, and we will be with him forever.

But the context indicates that Jesus is speaking of an *earlier* coming here: not just being with Jesus after he comes back in the future, but being with him in our daily lives in the present. How can this be?

Peter wants to follow Jesus wherever He goes, but Jesus tells him that if he wants to follow Jesus where He is going, he must follow Him to the death (John 13:31-38). Nevertheless, Peter and the other disciples should not be afraid; they should trust in Jesus the same way they trusted in the Father (14:1). He would prepare a dwelling-place for them in His Father's house, and would come back afterwards to receive them to Himself (14:2-3). "You know where I'm going and how I will get there," He told them (14:4). Perhaps like us, the disciples were confused, and Thomas spoke for all of them: "Lord, we don't even know where You're going; how can we know the way you're getting there?" (14:5) So Jesus clarifies His point: Where He is going to the Father (14:6), and He is going there by dying on the Cross but would return afterward to give them the Spirit (14:18-19; 16:18-22). How would they get to the Father? By coming through Jesus, who is the way (14:6).

We often cite John 14:2-3 as a proof-text for Jesus' future coming; conversely, we cite John 14:6 as a proof-text for salvation. But if we follow the flow of conversation, we have to be wrong about one of them. 14:2-3 declares that Jesus will bring them where He is going, but 14:6 tells us where He's going and how we His followers will get there: He is going to the Father, and we come to the Father when we get saved through Jesus (14:6). Do we come to the Father through Jesus only when He returns in the future, or have we come to Him already through faith? The entire context makes this point clear. We enter the Father's house when we become followers of Jesus Christ!

In the context of John's entire Gospel, there is no reason to assume that the "Father's house" refers to heaven, though it might be an allusion to the Temple (John 2:16) or to the Father's household (John 8:35; and we are His new temple and His household). More helpfully, Jesus goes on to explain the "dwelling-places" (NIV: "rooms") explicitly in the following context. The Greek word for "dwelling-place" used in 14:2 occurs in only one other verse in the New Testament—in this very context, in 14:23, part of Jesus' continuing explanation of 14:2-4. "The one who loves Me will obey Me, and My Father will love that one and we will come make our 'dwelling-place' with that person" (14:23). The related verb appears throughout John 15:1-10: "Dwell [abide]" in Christ, and let Christ "dwell" in you. We all know that Jesus will return someday in the future, but if we read the rest of John we learn that Jesus also returned to them from the Father after His resurrection, when He gave the disciples the Spirit, peace and joy (20:19-23), just as He had promised (14:16-17, 26-27; 16:20-22).

This is in fact the only coming the context addresses (14:18 in the context of 14:15-27; 16:12-24).

What is the real point of John 14:2-3? It is not that Jesus will return and we will be with Him someday—true as that teaching is from other texts. It is that Jesus returned after His resurrection so Christians could have life with Him (14:18-19), that He has already brought us into His presence and that we can experience the reality of His presence this very moment and at all times. This means that the same Jesus who washed his disciples feet in the preceding chapter, who taught and healed and suffered for us, is with us at this very moment. He invites us to trust His presence with us.

27. A Newborn Son in Isaiah 7:14

We are familiar with the New Testament use of the virgin-born son passage as a reference to Jesus in Matthew 1:23, but most of us have never considered how Matthew came to this conclusion. Matthew does not use all his Old Testament prophecies the same way. Some of Matthew's other Scripture texts refer in the Old Testament not to Jesus but to Israel; for instance, "out of Egypt I called My son" clearly refers to Israel's exodus from Egypt in Hosea 11:1, but Matthew applies it to Jesus' exodus from Egypt (Matt. 2:15). Matthew is not saying that Hosea had Jesus in mind; he is saying that Jesus as the ultimate son of Abraham (Matt. 1:1) recapitulates Israel's experiences (for instance, his forty days in the wilderness and His quotations from Deuteronomy in Matt. 4:1-11). That very chapter of Hosea goes on to speak of a new exodus, a new era of salvation comparable to the old one. Matthew quotes Hosea 11:1 because he knows that Hosea himself pointed to a future salvation.

So before we read Matthew's application of Isaiah 7:14 into Isaiah, we must carefully examine what Isaiah 7:14 means in context. (If this exercise makes you nervous, you can skip to our conclusion, but make sure you come back and follow our discussion the whole way through.) Although Matthew 1:23 clearly refers to Jesus being born of a virgin (the Greek term is clear), scholars dispute whether the Hebrew words in Isaiah also refer necessarily to a "virgin" or, more generally, to a "young woman." For the sake of argument, we will avoid this point and examine the context only.

The king of Assyria was encroaching on the boundaries of Israel (the kingdom of Samaria) and Syria (Aram, the kingdom of Damascus). Realizing that they were in trouble, they tried to get the king of Judah (the kingdom of Jerusalem) to join them in fighting the Assyrians. When he proved uncooperative, they sought to force him to join their coalition. At this time, God sent the prophet Isaiah to Ahaz, king of Judah, to warn him not to join the coalition of Israel and Syria. (Keep in mind that Judah and Israel were two separate countries by this point in their history.) Syria or Aram (represented by its capital Damascus) and Israel or Ephraim (represented by Samaria) would be crushed shortly (7:4-9).

Isaiah even offered the Judean king Ahaz a sign to confirm that Aram and Israel would quickly fall (7:10-13). The sign was one that would get Ahaz's attention: a woman would bear a son and name him Immanuel, "God is with us" (7:14). Before the son would know right from wrong, while still eating curds (7:15; this was in Isaiah's day, 7:21-25), the Assyrian king would devastate Aram and Israel (7:16-20). In other words, the child would be born in Ahaz's generation! But then, why was the son named, "God is with us"? Perhaps for the same reason that all Isaiah's children bore symbolic names (8:18), just as Hosea's children were prophetic signs to the northern kingdom of Israel in roughly the same period (Hosea 2:4-9). We will come back to this point later in our discussion.

After offering this prophecy to Ahaz, Isaiah was sent in to "the prophetess" (presumably his young, new wife, who may have also had the gift of prophecy) and she got pregnant. They named the son "Mahershalalhashbaz"—"Swift is the booty, speedy is the prey." God said to name the child this as a sign to Judah that God would quickly give Judah's enemies into the hands of the Assyrian army. Before the boy was old enough to utter the most childish form of, "Mother" or "Father," Assyria would plunder Aram and Israel (8:1-10). In other words, Isaiah's own son would be the sign to Ahaz: his birth would be quickly followed by the devastation of the lands to the north that had sought to force Judah into their coalition. Judah needed to know that "God is with us," and that Aram's and Israel's "booty" would be carried away "speedily," and its "prey...swiftly" (7:14; 8:3).

So why did Matthew think Isaiah 7:14 could be applied to Jesus? Probably not for the same reason we often do. We apply Isaiah 7:14 to Jesus because we never read its immediate context; Matthew probably applied it to Jesus because he read past the immediate context to the broader context of surrounding passages. As we mentioned before, Isaiah's children were for "signs," each teaching Judah of what God would do (8:18). The immediate sign of God being with Judah would be the conquest of their enemies to the north; but the ultimate act of God being with them would be when God Himself actually came to be with them. In the very next passage, Isaiah announces a hope that would extend beyond Judah even to the northern kingdom of Israel (9:1-2), a conquering king, a child who would be born to the house of Judah (9:3-7). Not only would He be *called* "God is with us"; like his other titles, which appropriately apply to Him, "Mighty God" would apply to Him (9:6, a title of God also found in the context, 10:21). This Davidic King (9:7) would be God in the flesh (9:6); in the ancient near East, where Israel may have been unusual for not turning its kings into gods, Isaiah certainly would not have risked calling this king "Mighty God" if he had not meant that God Himself was coming to reign as one of David's descendants. Matthew was right, but not for the reason we would have assumed!

Some critics of Matthew, who believe that he simply did not know the context, are skeptical. It is fair to point out to them that Matthew demonstrates his knowledge of the context just three chapters later. There he applies to Jesus a passage from Isaiah 9:1-2 (Matt 4:15-16), showing that the context of Isaiah 7:14 remains fresh in his mind!

As we have seen, context dramatically affects the way we interpret each passage. But in most cases context must go beyond the surrounding paragraph to surrounding chapters or even the entire book in which a passage occurs. Thus we turn in the next chapter to a discussion of a larger level of context in which many readers are not yet skilled.

Chapter 3
Whole-Book Context

While it is important to read each passage in the context that immediately surrounds it, it is also important to read it in the context of the entire book in which it appears—whether John or Judges or James or other books of the Bible. This is the way God gave us most of the Bible, inspiring particular authors to write books, which the first readers received one book at a time.

Often the particular passage we are studying fits into an argument that runs through that entire book of the Bible. Often points in our passage develop themes that run through that book; viewed in light of how the book treats that theme elsewhere, the points in our passage become much clearer. In some cases, the story runs over several books in our Bible that were once connected as extended narratives (for instance, the Moses story in Exodus carries over from the Joseph story in Genesis, and 1 Samuel through 2 Kings are one long story; so also is Luke plus Acts).

A concordance can help you see how given words are used elsewhere in the same book; you can practice this by tracing the word "law" or "Spirit" through Galatians. If you want to develop this skill more fully, instead of using a concordance, simply read through Galatians and make your own list of some themes, and references of the verses where each theme appears.

Following are some examples of how reading a passage in light of the book where it occurs enriches our understanding of the passage.

1. Jewish-Gentile Reconciliation in Romans

We often urge people to be converted by believing in Jesus' resurrection with their heart and confessing with their mouth that Jesus is Lord. This summary of how to respond to the gospel is based on Romans 10:9-10, which does in fact discuss salvation. But it is helpful to examine why Paul specifically mentions the mouth and heart here (rather than in some other passages which emphasize different aspects of salvation). Certainly Paul would not deny that a deaf mute could be saved simply because they could not confess with their mouth. He chooses the particular words "heart" and "mouth" for specific reasons evident in the context.

We look first at the immediate context, as we did in passages above. Paul believes that we are saved by God's grace, not by our works. Contrary to the means of justification proposed by Paul's opponents (Rom. 10:1-5), Paul demonstrates from the law of Moses itself that the message of faith is the saving word (10:6-7). As Moses said, "the word is near you, in your mouth and in your heart" (10:8); Moses was referring to the law (Deut 30:10-11, 14), but the principle was also applicable to the gospel, which was also God's word. In Moses' day one could not ascend to heaven to bring the law down from above; God in his mercy already gave it to Israel on Mount Sinai (30:12). Nor was it necessary to descend again into the sea (30:13); God had already redeemed his people and brought them through the sea. They could not save themselves; they had to depend on God's mighty grace (cf. Ex 20:2). In the same way, Paul says, we don't bring Christ up from the dead, or send him down from the Father; like the law and Israel's redemption, Christ's salvation is God's gift to us (Rom 10:6-7). Moses declared that this message was "in your mouth and in your heart" (Deut 30:14), i.e., already given to Israel by God's grace. Paul explains that likewise God's message was in your mouth when you confessed Christ with your mouth and in your heart when you believed in Him in your heart (Rom 10:9-10). Faith could come only from hearing this word, the gospel of Christ (10:17), as we noted above.

The immediate context explains why Paul mentions the "mouth" and the "heart" in this specific passage, but it also raises a new question. Why did Paul have to make an argument from the Old Testament that salvation was by grace through faith? Was there anyone who doubted this? Reading Romans as an entire book explains the reason for each passage within that book. Paul is addressing a controversy between Jewish and Gentile Christians.

Paul begins Romans by emphasizing that the Gentiles are lost (Rom 1:18-32); just as the Jewish Christian readers are applauding, Paul points out that religious people are also lost (Rom 2), and summarizes that everyone is lost (Rom 3). Paul establishes that all humanity is equally lost to remind us that all of us have to come to God on the same terms; none of us can boast against others.

But most Jewish people believed that they were chosen for salvation in Abraham; therefore Paul reminds his fellow Jewish Christians that it is spiritual rather than ethnic descent from Abraham that matters for salvation (Rom 4). Lest any of his Jewish readers continue to stress their genetic descent, he reminds them that all people--including themselves--descend from sinful Adam (5:12-21). Jewish people believed that most Jews kept all 613 commandments in the law (at least most of the time), whereas most Gentiles did not even keep the seven commandments many Jews believed God gave to Noah. So Paul argues that while the law is good, it never saved its practitioners, including Paul (Rom 7); only Jesus Christ could do that!

And lest the Jewish Christians continue to insist on their chosenness in Abraham, Paul reminds them that not all Abraham's physical descendants were chosen, even in the first two generations (Rom 9:6-13). God was so sovereign, he was not bound to choosing people on the basis of their ethnicity (9:18-24); he could choose people on the basis of their faith in Christ.

But lest the Gentile Christians look down on the Jewish Christians, Paul also reminds them that the heritage into which they had been grafted was, after all, Israel's (Rom 11). God had a Jewish remnant, and would one day turn the majority of Jewish people to faith in Christ (11:25-26). And at this point Paul gets very practical. Christians must serve one another (Rom 12); the heart of God's law is actually loving one another (13:8-10). Ancient literature shows that Roman Gentiles made fun of Roman Jews especially for their food laws and holy days; Paul argues that we should not look down on one another because of such minor differences of practice (Rom 14). He then provides examples of ethnic reconciliation: Jesus though Jewish ministered to the Gentiles (15:7-12) and Paul was bringing an offering from Gentile churches for the Jewish Christians in Jerusalem (15:25-31). In the midst of his closing greetings, he offers one final exhortation: Beware of those who cause division (16:17).

Getting the whole picture of Romans provides us a clearer understanding of the function of each particular passage in the work as a whole. It also suggests the sort of situation which the letter addresses. What we know of the "background" sheds more light on this situation: Rome earlier expelled the Jewish Christians (Acts 18:1-3), but now they have returned (Rom 16:3). This means that the Roman house churches, which had consisted completely of Gentiles for many years, now face conflict with Jewish Christians who had different cultural ways of doing things. Paul's letter to the Romans summons Christians to ethnic, cultural, tribal reconciliation with one another by reminding us that all of us came to God on the same terms, through Jesus Christ alone. (But we will turn to the issue of background more fully later.)

2. Justice for the Poor in James

Some people, reading the letter of James, have thought that the letter collects miscellaneous exhortations that do not fit together very well. But their view is unlikely: when one examines James carefully, most of the book actually fits together quite well.

In the "immediate context" section above, we asked how James expected us to resist the devil (4:7), and argued that he referred to resisting the world's values. This is a valid general principle, but were there any specific values that James was especially concerned about among his readers? Most likely, there were.

In the introduction to James' letter he introduces several themes which recur through the rest of the letter. By tracing these themes, we get a simple outline of the basic issues the letter addresses. (When I preach on James, I often like to preach from the introduction of the letter, which allows me to actually preach most of the letter using just one or two paragraphs as my outline.)

First of all, we see the problem James confronts: his readers encounter various trials (1:2). As one reads through the letter, one gathers that many of his readers are poor people who are being oppressed by the rich (1:9-11; 2:2-6; 5:1-6). (Background sheds even more light on this situation, which was very common in James's day. But for now we will continue to focus on whole-book context, since we will do more with background later.) Some of James' readers appear tempted to deal with their problem of various trials in the wrong way: with a violent (whether verbally or physically) response (1:19-20; 2:11; 3:9; 4:2).

So James offers a solution demanding from them three virtues: endurance (1:3-4), wisdom (1:5), and faith (1:6-8). They need God's wisdom to properly endure, and they need faith when they pray to God for this wisdom. James returns to each of these virtues later in his letter, explaining them in further detail. Thus he deals with endurance more fully near the end of his letter, using Job and the prophets as biblical examples of such endurance (5:7-11). He also demands sincere rather than merely passing faith (2:14-26). What he says about faith here is instructive. Some of the poor were tempted to lash out and kill their oppressors, and might think God would still be on their side so long as they had not committed sins like adultery. But James reminds them that murder is sin even if they do not commit adultery (2:11). The basic confession of Jewish faith was the oneness of God, but James reminds his friends that even the devil had "faith" that God was one, but this knowledge did not save the devil (2:19). Genuine faith means faith that is demonstrated by obedience (2:14-18). Thus if we pray "in faith" for wisdom, we must pray in the genuine faith that is willing to obey whatever wisdom God gives us! We must not be "double-minded" (1:8), which means trying to embrace both the world's perspective and God's at the same time (4:8).

James especially treats in more detail the matter of wisdom. He is concerned about inflammatory rhetoric--the sort of speech that stirs people to anger against others (1:19-20; 3:1-12). This does not mean that he remains silent toward rich oppressors; he prophesies God's judgment against them (5:1-6)! But he does not approve of stirring people to violence against them. James notes that there are two kinds of wisdom. One kind involves strife and selfishness and is worldly and demonic (3:14); this is the sort of view and attitude which tempts his readers. James instead advocates God's way of wisdom, which is gentle (3:13); it is pure--unmixed with other kinds of wisdom--and peaceable, gentle, easily entreated, full of mercy and the fruit of righteousness which is sown in peace (3:17-18). His readers were tempted to use violence (4:2) and desire the world's way of doing things (4:4). But rather than taking matters into their own hands, they should submit to God (4:7).

James is calling us to keep peace with one another. And if he calls the oppressed not to seek to kill their oppressors, how much more does he summon all of us to love and remain gentle toward those closest to us, even those who are unkind to us? "Resisting the devil" may involve more work than some people think!

3. David's Judgment in 2 Samuel 12:11

Sometimes we think that David's punishment ended with his son's death (12:18). But because David was a leader in God's household, his behavior affected many others and required strict judgment (12:14); God takes sin very seriously, especially when it leads others to misunderstand his holiness. In 12:11, Nathan prophesies against David judgment from within his household, including the rape of some his wives (as he committed immorality with another man's wife) by a friend of his, in public. This prophecy provides almost an outline for the rest of 2 Samuel!

In chapter 13, David's son Amnon rapes his half-sister Tamar. Tamar's full brother Absalom avenges his sister's honor by killing Amnon--who also happens to be the brother immediately his elder, meaning that--if Chileab is uninvolved in politics (he is nowhere mentioned)--Absalom is also next in line for the throne by birthright (2 Sam 3:2-3). Absalom returns from exile (ch. 14), and then leads a revolt that nearly destroyed David and his allies (chs. 15-18)--and broke his father's heart. Absalom slept with his father's concubines in the sight of Israel (16:21), despite the fact that this was against the law (Lev 20:11). Once this revolt was quelled and David returned to Jerusalem in peace (ch. 19), he had to deal with another revolt in the wake of the previous one, by a Benjamite usurper (ch. 20). By the opening of 1 Kings, the son immediately younger than Absalom is plotting to seize the throne (1 Kgs 1). Though forgiven by God and restored to his throne, David suffered the consequences of his pattern of sin for the rest of his life. This story provides a harsh warning for spiritual leaders today who forget their responsibility to live holy lives.

4. The "least of these" in Matt 25:40

Many people today emphasize the importance of caring for the poor by reminding us that Jesus warned us we would be judged by how we treat "the least of these" Jesus' brothers (25:40, 45). While it is true that God will judge us according to how we treat the poor, is the "poor" what Jesus means here by his "brothers"? Will the nations be judged (25:32) only for this? The immediate context does not settle the issue, but the broader context of the Gospel tradition may help more. What does Jesus mean elsewhere by "brothers" and by the "least"?

Because ancient readers would unwind a scroll from the beginning, the first readers would have already read the preceding chapters before coming to Matthew 25. Thus they would know that Jesus' brothers and sisters included all those who did his will (Matt 12:48-50), that all Jesus' disciples are brothers and sisters (23:8), and, before they finished the Gospel, would know that Jesus' disciples remained his brothers after his resurrection (28:10). (Because of the way the Greek language works, "brothers" often can include "sisters" as well, but in 28:10 the women disciples are addressing specifically the men disciples.) When Jesus speaks of the "least" in the kingdom, he sometimes also refers to some disciples (11:11).

Who then are the least of these disciples of Jesus that the nations accepted or rejected? It is at least possible that these are messengers of the gospel, "missionaries," who bring the gospel to all unreached people groups before the day of judgment; certainly the message about the kingdom would be spread among all those people groups before the kingdom would come (24:14). These messengers might be hungry and thirsty because of the comforts they sacrificed to bring others the gospel; they might be imprisoned because of persecution; they might even be worn down to sickness by their efforts (like Epaphroditus in Phil 2:27-30). But those who received such messengers would receive Jesus who sent them, even if all they had to give them was a cup of cold water to drink--as Jesus had taught earlier (10:11-14, 40-42). It is possible, then, in light of the entire Gospel of Matthew, that these "least brothers and sisters" are the lowliest of the missionaries sent to the nations; the nations will be judged according to how they respond to Jesus' emissaries.

5. What it means to Believe in John 3:16

John 3:16 does refer to salvation from sin through faith in Jesus, as we usually expect. But we do not catch the full meaning of this verse unless we read the Gospel of John the whole way through. The rest of the Gospel sheds light on what this verse means about the "world" (for instance, it includes Samaritans--see 4:42 in context), on how God expressed his love (by describing the cross), and other issues. We focus here on what John 3:16 means by saving faith. Someone may say he believes in Jesus, yet this person may attend church once a year and continue to live in unrepentant sin (let us say this person murders people every other weekend). Is this person really a Christian? What does it really mean to "believe" in Jesus?

The rest of the Gospel of John clarifies what Jesus means here by saving faith. Just before the conversation in which Jesus speaks 3:16, John tells us about some inadequate believers. Many people were impressed with Jesus' miracles and "believed" in him, but Jesus refused to put his faith in them because he knew what was really inside them (2:23-25). They had some sort of faith, but it was not saving faith.

What would happen if someone professed faith in Christ, then later renounced Christ and became a Muslim or worshiped old Yoruba gods? Would their earlier profession of faith be enough to save them in the end? The question is not hard to answer in light of the rest of John's Gospel, though some of us may not like the answer. Later in the Gospel of John, some of Jesus' hearers "believed" in him, but he warned them that they must continue in his word, so proving to be his disciples and learning the truth which would free them (8:30-32). By the end of the chapter, however, these hearers have already proved unfaithful: they actually want to kill Jesus (8:59). Jesus later warns that those who fail to continue in him will be cast away (15:4, 6). In John's Gospel, genuine saving faith is the kind of faith that perseveres to the end.

The purpose of John's Gospel was to record some of his signs for Christian readers who had never seen Jesus in person, that they might come to a deeper level of faith, the kind of faith that would be strong enough to persevere in following Jesus to the end (20:30-31). John makes this comment right after narrating the climactic confession of faith in this Gospel. Jesus summons Thomas to "believe," and Thomas expresses his faith by calling Jesus, "My Lord and my God" (20:27-28). Jesus' deity is an emphasis in John's Gospel (1:1, 18; 8:58), so of all the other confessions about Jesus' identity in this Gospel (1:29, 36, 49; 6:69), this is the climactic one: He is God. The content of Thomas's faith is correct, but John wants more from his own readers. Correct information about Jesus is necessary, but by itself correct information is not necessarily strong faith. Thomas believed because he saw, but Jesus says that he wants greater faith that can believe even before it sees (20:29). John's readers believe because he narrates his eyewitness testimony to them (20:30-31), confirmed by the power of the Holy Spirit (15:26-16:15).

In John 3:16, saving faith is not just praying a single prayer, then going on our way and forgetting about Jesus for the rest of our lives. Saving faith is embracing Jesus with such radical dependence on his work for us that we stake our lives on the truth of his claims.

6. Under the Law in Romans 7

Earlier we noted the importance of the entire structure of Romans, whih teaches us about ethnic reconciliation. In this context, the specific function of Romans 7 is significant: Paul notes that believers are no longer "under the law" (7:1-6). But he also notes that the problem is not with the law itself (7:7, 12, 14), but with humans as creatures of "flesh." Many people take this chapter as also depicting Paul's present enslavement to sin, and some even use it to justify living sinfully, saying, "If Paul could not keep from living in sin, how can we?" Is that really Paul's point?

In 7:14, Paul declares that he is "fleshly, sold into slavery to sin." In surrounding chapters, however, he declares that all believers in Jesus have been freed from sin and made slaves to God and righteousness (6:18-22). In 7:18, Paul complains that "nothing good dwells" in him, but in 8:9 he explains that the Spirit of Christ dwells in all true believers. In 7:25 he confesses that he serves with his body the "law of sin"; but in 8:2 he declares that Jesus has freed believers from "the law of sin and death."

Why this apparent confusion? Probably only because we have missed the primary issue. Although Paul speaks graphically about life under the law in Romans 7, he is not implying that this is his typical daily Christian life. He says that when believers "were" in the flesh (probably meaning, ruled by their own desires), their sinful passions stirred by the law were producing death in them. By contrast, Paul says, "But now" believers have been "freed from the law," serving instead by the Spirit (7:5-6). That is, most of Romans 7 depicts the frustration of trying to achieve righteousness by the works of the law, that is, by human effort (Rom 7 speaks of "I," "me," "my" and "mine" over forty times). When we accept the righteousness of God as a free gift in Jesus Christ, however, we become able to walk in newness of life, and the rest of the Christian life is daring to trust the finished work of Christ enough to live like it is so (6:11). To the extent that our lives resemble Romans 7 at all, it is because we are trying to make ourselves good enough for God instead of accepting His gracious love for us.

7. Reproving Loveless Christians in 1 Corinthians 13

We often quote 1 Corinthians 13 as if it is an all-purpose description of love, for weddings, marriage counseling, friendships, and so forth. The principles in this chapter are in fact universal enough to apply to those situations, but Paul originally wrote them to address a specific situation which many of us today miss. Paul was addressing the appropriate use of spiritual gifts.

The Corinthian church was divided over a variety of issues. One such issue, addressed in chapters 12-14, was the use of some spiritual gifts. Paul reminds the Christians in Corinth that the purpose of all publicly used gifts is to build up the body of Christ. In chapter

14, he emphasizes that prophecy is more important in public worship than tongues, because it builds up the church better (unless the tongues is interpreted). Between these two chapters is chapter 13, revealing love as the key virtue that moves us to use all our gifts to build up Christ's church.

Paul emphasizes that even if we have the greatest gifts, we are nothing without love (13:1-3). He points out that the gifts are temporary, due to pass away at Christ's return when we see him face to face (13:8-10); love, however, is eternal (13:11-13). Between these two points he describes the characteristics of love--characteristics which, in the context of the entire book, directly address what the Corinthian Christians lack (13:4-8). Love is not jealous or arrogant or boastful (13:4), but the Corinthian Christians certainly were jealous (3:3) and arrogant (4:6, 18-19; 5:2; 8:1) and boastful (cf. 1:29; 3:21; 4:7; 5:6). In short, everything Paul says love is, he has already told the Corinthians they are not! Paul's praise of love is simultaneously a gentle rebuke!

But just as love is our first priority, love tells us which gifts to seek most for the building up of Christ's body. The verses immediately surrounding 1 Corinthians 13 remind us that we should seek from God for public worship especially the "greater" gifts, those like prophecy which build up others (12:31; 14:1).

8. The Spirit-baptized life in Mk 1:8-13

The Gospel of Mark explicitly mentions God's Spirit only six times, but half of them appear in his introduction (1:8-13), where he introduces several of his central themes for his audience. His other uses emphasize the Spirit's work in empowering Jesus for exorcism (Mk 3:29-30), Old Testament prophets to speak God's message (12:26) or Jesus' witnesses to speak his message (13:11).

In the introduction, John the Baptist announces the mighty one who will baptize others in the Holy Spirit (1:8); this Spirit-baptizer is Jesus of Nazareth. Immediately after this announcement, we see Jesus baptized and the Spirit coming on him (1:9-10). The Spirit-baptizer thus gives us a model of what the Spirit-baptized life will look like, for he himself receives the Spirit first. That is why what the Spirit does next appears all the more stunning: the Spirit thrusts Jesus into the wilderness for conflict with the devil (1:12-13). The Spirit-filled life is not a life of ease and comfort, but of conflict with the devil's forces!

The rest of the Gospel of Mark continues this pattern. Shortly after Jesus emerges from the wilderness, he must confront an evil spirit in a religious gathering (1:21-27). Throughout the rest of the Gospel, Jesus continues to defeat the devil by healing the sick and driving out demons (cf. 3:27), while the devil continues to strike at Jesus through the devil's religious and political agents. In the end, the devil manages to get Jesus killed--but Jesus triumphs by rising from the dead.

In the same way, Jesus expects his disciples to heal the sick and drive out demons (3:14-15; 4:40; 6:13; 9:19, 28-29; 11:22-24), and also to join him in suffering (8:34-38; 10:29-31, 38-40; 13:9-13). His disciples seemed more happy to share his triumphs than his sufferings, but the Gospel of Mark emphasizes that we cannot share his glory without also sharing his suffering. That lesson remains as relevant for modern disciples as for ancient ones!

9. How to Make Disciples in Matthew 28:18-20

The immediate context of 28:18-20 provides us examples for how to testify about Christ (28:1-10) and how *not* to testify about Christ (28:11-15). But the context of the whole Gospel of Matthew further informs how we should read this passage, especially because it is the conclusion of the Gospel and readers would have finished the rest of this Gospel by the time they reach it.

The command to "make disciples" of all nations (KJV has "teach" them) is surrounded by three clauses in Greek that describe how we make disciples of the nations: by "going," "baptizing," and "teaching." Jesus had spoken of "going" when he had sent his disciples out even within Galilee (10:7), but here disciples must go to other cultures and peoples because they will make disciples of the "nations."

Making disciples of the "nations" fits an emphasis developed throughout this Gospel. The four women specifically mentioned in Jesus' ancestry (1:2-17) appear to be Gentiles: Tamar the Canaanite, Rahab the Jerichoite, Ruth the Moabitess, and the "widow of Uriah" the Hittite (1:3, 5-6). Ancient Jewish genealogies normally emphasized the purity of one's Israelite lineage, but this genealogy deliberately underlines the mixed-race heritage of the Messiah who will save Gentiles as well as Jews.

When many of his own people ignored or persecuted him, pagan astrologers from the East came to worship him (2:1-12). God and his Son could raise up Abraham's children even from stones (3:9), work in "Galilee of the Gentiles" (4:15), bless the faith of a Roman military officer (8:5-13), deliver demoniacs in Gentile territory (8:28-34), compare Israelite cities unfavorably with Sodom (10:15; 11:23-24), reward the persistent faith of a Canaanite woman (15:21-28), allow the first apostolic confession of Jesus' Messiahship in pagan territory (16:13), promise that all nations would hear the gospel (24:14), and allow the first confession of Jesus as God's Son after the cross to come from a Roman execution squad (27:54). Matthew probably

wrote to encourage his fellow Jewish Christians to
evangelize the Gentiles, so the Gospel fittingly closes
on this command.

"Baptizing" recalls the mission of John the
Baptist, who baptized people for repentance (3:1-2, 6,
11). Baptism in Jewish culture represented an act of
conversion, so as "going" may represent crosscultural
ministry, we may describe Jesus' command to "baptize"
as evangelism. But evangelism is not sufficient to
make full disciples; we also need Christian education.
"Teaching" them all that Jesus commanded is made
easier by the fact that Matthew has provided us Jesus'
teachings conveniently in five major discourse sections:
Jesus' teachings about the ethics of the kingdom (chs.
5-7); proclaiming the kingdom (ch. 10); parables about
the present state of the kingdom (ch. 13); relationships
in the kingdom (ch. 18); and the future of the kingdom
and judgment on the religious establishment (chs. 23-
25).

But in Matthew's Gospel, we do not make
disciples the way most Jewish teachers in his day made
disciples. We make disciples not for ourselves but for
our Lord Jesus Christ (23:8). This final paragraph of
Matthew's Gospel fittingly concludes various themes
about Jesus' identity in this Gospel as well. John (3:2),
Jesus (4:17), and his followers (10:7) announced God's
kingdom, his reign; now Jesus reigns with all authority
in all creation (28:18). Further, we baptize not only in

the name of God and his Spirit, but in the name of
Jesus (28:19), thereby ranking Jesus as deity alongside
the Father and the Spirit. And finally, Jesus' promise to
be with us always as we preach the kingdom until the
end of the age (28:20) recalls earlier promises in the
Gospel. Jesus himself is "Immanuel," "God with us"
(1:23), and wherever two or three gather in his name
he will be among them (18:20). To any ancient Jewish
reader, these statements would imply that Jesus was
God.

Does the promise that Jesus will be with us "till
the end of the age" (28:20) imply that once the age
ends he will no longer be with us? Such an idea would
miss entirely the point of the text. Jesus is promising
to be with us in carrying out his commission (28:19);
that must be accomplished before the age ends (24:14),
so the nations can be judged according to how they
have responded to this message (25:31-32). Taking this
passage in the context of the entire Gospel provides
us plenty of preaching material without even stepping
outside Matthew!

10. Loyalty to the Death in John 13:34-35

When Jesus commands us to love one
another as he has loved us, why does he call this a
"new" commandment (13:34)? Did not God command
all believers to love one another even in the Old
Testament (Lev 19:18). What makes this commandment

a new commandment is the new example set by the Lord Jesus.

The immediate context makes this example clearer. Jesus takes the role of a humble servant by washing his disciples' feet (13:1-11); he also calls on his disciples to imitate his servanthood (13:12-17). In the same context, we understand the degree to which he became a servant for us by noting what he would suffer: Jesus and the narrator keep talking about Jesus' impending betrayal (13:11, 18-30). Jesus explains that he is being "glorified" (13:31-32), i.e., killed (12:23-24); he is about to leave the disciples (13:33), and Peter is not yet spiritually prepared to follow Jesus in martyrdom (13:36-38). This is the context of loving one another "as" Jesus loved us. We are called to sacrifice even our lives for one another!

The rest of the Gospel of John illustrates more fully Jesus' example of love and servanthood which culminates in the cross.

11. Judah's Punishment in Genesis 38

In his attacks on Christianity, South African writer Ahmed Deedat complains that the Bible is full of pornography and that Genesis 38, the story of Judah and Tamar, is a "filthy, dirty story." Did the Bible include this story simply to satisfy base interests of ungodly readers? Or have Deedat and others missed the entire point of the story?

The story can be summarized briefly, after which we will quickly see a moral lesson in it. Judah has three sons, Er (38:3), Onan (38:4), and Shelah (38:5). When God killed Er for sinful behavior (38:7), his younger brother Onan automatically inherited Er's responsibility to raise up offspring for his brother's name. Some cultures where women cannot earn money practice widow inheritance, where another brother takes over the deceased brother's wife. In the cultures around this family, however, normally a brother would simply get the widow pregnant, so that she could have a son who would receive her first husband's share of the inheritance; this son would in turn support her in her old age.

But Onan spills his seed on the ground, and God angrily strikes him dead (38:9-10), as he had struck his brother before him. Why did Onan "spill his seed"? And what was so sinful about him doing so? The firstborn (in this case Er) normally received twice as much inheritance as any other brother; if Onan raised up a son for his brother, that son would be counted as his brother's son and would receive half the inheritance, leaving only a quarter for Onan and a quarter for Shelah. But if Tamar could not become pregnant, Onan would receive two-thirds of the inheritance and Shelah one-third. Onan was greedy, and cared more about the extra inheritance than about honoring his brother and providing for Tamar. God defended Tamar's honor, because he cared about Tamar. The text teaches us about justice.

But the story goes on. Judah, fearing that allowing his sons to sleep with Tamar is leading to their deaths, refuses to give his final son to Tamar. In some of the surrounding cultures (though never in later Israelite law), if a brother were unavailable, a father was considered acceptable; so Tamar takes matters into her own hands. She disguises herself as a prostitute, knowing what kind of person Judah is; then she allows him to impregnate her, but keeps his signet ring so she can later prove that he is the father (38:18).

When Judah learns that Tamar is pregnant, he orders her to be executed. This reflects a double standard practiced in many cultures: the idea that a man can have sex with anyone (as Judah slept with what he thought was a prostitute) but a woman cannot. But God has no double standard: sin is as wrong for a man as it is for a woman. Tamar sent him the signet ring, forcing Judah to release her and admit, "She is more righteous than I" (38:26). That was the moral of the story: Judah was immoral and raised two immoral sons, and now is caught in his guilt. By challenging the double standard of his culture, the writer argues against sin. This is not a "dirty story" at all!

But whole-book context shows us more. The chapter directly before chapter 38 is chapter 37, where Judah takes the lead in selling his brother Joseph into slavery. In chapter 38, Judah's lifestyle of sin finally catches up with him, and he suffers for it! He sold his father's son into slavery; now he loses two of his own sons to death. The chapter after 38 is chapter 39, where Joseph resists the sexual advances of Potipher's wife, despite the penalty he faces for doing so. Joseph does not practice a double standard: he lives holy no matter what the cost. And a few chapters later, God rewards Joseph for his obedience; he becomes Pharaoh's vizier, and the agent through whom God can actually rescue the very brothers who sold him into slavery. And when Joseph is exalted, Pharaoh gives Joseph his signet-ring (41:42)--inviting us to remember Judah who lent his to what he thought was a prostitute (38:11). The larger story has a moral: those who live sinful lifestyles may prosper in the short run, but eventually they suffer; by contrast, those who remain faithful to God may suffer at first, but in the end they will be blessed.

This, however, is not the end of the story. Although Judah took the lead in selling his half-brother Joseph into slavery, Judah learned from his mistakes. Later he takes responsibility for Joseph's full brother Benjamin before their father Jacob (43:8-9), and for his father's sake takes responsibility for Benjamin before Joseph (44:16-34). Judah is ready to become a slave himself to keep Benjamin from becoming one--and this is what convinces Joseph that his brothers finally have changed. The final moral of the story, then, is one of forgiveness and reconciliation, and the faithfulness of God who arranged events to bring it all about. Ahmed Deedat did not read far enough to understand the story!

12. Rivers of Living Water in John 7:37-38

Jesus' promise of rivers of living water in John 7:37-38, referring to the coming of the Holy Spirit (7:39), is exciting in any case. But it is especially exciting if one traces through the rest of the Gospel the contrast between the true water of the Spirit and merely ritual uses of water by Jesus' contemporaries.

John's baptism in water was good, but Jesus' baptism in the Spirit was better (1:26, 33). Strict Jewish ritual required the waterpots in Cana to be used only for ritual waters to purify, but when Jesus turned the water into wine he showed that he valued his friend's honor more than ritual and tradition (2:6). A Samaritan woman abandons her waterpot used to draw water from the sacred ancestral well when she realizes that Jesus offers new water that brings eternal life (4:13-14). A sick man unable to be healed by water that supposedly brought healing (5:7) finds healing instead in Jesus (5:8-9); a blind man is healed by water in some sense but only because Jesus "sends" him there (9:7).

The function of this water is suggested more fully in John 3:5. Here Jesus explains that Nicodemus cannot understand God's kingdom without being born "from above" (3:3, literally), i.e., from God. Some Jewish teachers spoke of Gentiles being "reborn" in a sense when they converted to Judaism, but Nicodemus cannot conceive of himself as a Gentile, a pagan, so he assumes Jesus speaks instead of reentering his mother's womb (3:4). So Jesus clarifies his statement. Jewish people believed that Gentiles converted to Judaism through circumcision and baptism, so Jesus explains to Nicodemus that he must be reborn "from water." In other words, Nicodemus must come to God on the same terms that Gentiles do!

But if Jesus means by "water" here what he means in 7:37-38, he may mean water as a symbol for the Spirit, in which case he is saying, "You must be born of water, i.e., the Spirit" (a legitimate way to read the Greek). If so, Jesus may be using Jewish conversion baptism merely to symbolize the greater baptism in the Spirit that he brings to those who trust in him. The water may also symbolize Jesus' sacrificial servanthood for his disciples (13:5).

So what does Jesus mean by the rivers of living water in John 7:37-38? Even though we will deal with background and translations more fully later, we need to use them at least briefly here to catch the full impact of this passage. First, in most current translations, at least a footnote points out an alternate way to punctuate 7:37-38 (the earliest Greek texts lacked punctuation, and the early church fathers divided over which interpretation to take). In this other way to read the verses, it is not clear that the water flows from the believer; it may flow instead from Christ. Since believers "receive" rather than give the water (7:39), and since they elsewhere have a "well" rather than a "river" (4:14), Christ may well be the source of water in these verses. (This is not to deny the possibility that believers may experience deeper empowerments of the Spirit after their conversion.)

Jewish tradition suggests that on the last day of the Feast of Tabernacles, priests read to the people from Zechariah 14 and Ezekiel 47, which talk of rivers of living water flowing forth from the Temple in the end time. Jesus is now speaking on the last day of that feast (7:2, 37), probably alluding to the very Scriptures from which they had read ("as the Scripture said," 7:38). Jewish people thought of the Temple as the "navel" or "belly" of the earth. So Jesus may be declaring, "I am the foundation stone of the new temple of God. From me flows the water of the river of life; let the one who wills come and drink freely!"

Normally (as we will point out below) one should not read symbolism into biblical narratives, but the end of John's Gospel may be an exception, a symbol God provided those who watched the crucifixion. (John uses symbolism a little more than narratives normally do.) When a soldier pierced Jesus' side, water as well as blood flowed forth (19:34). Literally, a spear thrust near the heart could release a watery fluid around the heart as well as blood. But John is the only writer among the four Gospel writers to emphasize the water, and he probably mentions it to make a point: once Jesus was lifted up on the cross and glorified (7:39), the new life of the Spirit became available to his people. Let us come and drink freely.

13. Moses' Character in Exodus 6:10-30

Most of us do not preach from genealogies; most individual genealogies were probably not designed exactly for preaching anyway. But one must ask why God suddenly interrupts the story of Moses with a genealogy in Exodus 6:14-25. God commands Moses to tell Pharaoh to release his people, but Moses protests that his own people have not heeded him, so how would Pharaoh listen to him (6:10-13)? After the genealogy, the narrative repeats the point: God commands Moses to confront Pharaoh, and Moses protests that Pharaoh will not listen to him.

What is the point of interrupting this narrative with a genealogy? The genealogy itself lists three tribes, the three oldest tribes, which sages who remembered the story might have called out until getting to Moses' tribe. But the fact that the genealogy occurs at this point in the narrative may indicate more than that. The list reminds us that Moses was descended from Levi, and related to Reuben and Simeon. Reuben slept with his father's concubine and Simeon and Levi massacred all the men in Shechem. By placing the genealogy here, Exodus may be commenting on why Moses was so uncomfortable with confronting Pharaoh. If he was descended from such people as Levi, Reuben and Simeon, is it any wonder that Moses would act like this?

With the exception of Jesus, all the people God chose in the Bible were people with weaknesses rather than those who might think they "deserved" to be called. God chose broken people whose triumphs would bring glory to him rather than to themselves.

14. Rebekah's Deceit (Gen 27:5-10)

Some readers have accused both Isaac and Rebekah of equal fault in favoring their sons (Esau and Jacob respectively; Gen 27:1-10). But in context of the entire book of Genesis, the motives of the two parents are quite different. Isaac favors the elder son (25:25; 27:4), but the whole patriarchal line suggests that God does not always choose the elder son (21:12; 49:3-4), and paternal favoritism produces problems (37:4); Jacob himself finally learns and practices this in his old age (48:14-20). What are Rebekah's motives? The clearest clue the text itself provides is in 25:22-23:

she had sought God, and God had told her that the younger would prevail. In contrast to Isaac, Rebekah acts on the basis of a word from God. Further, Esau had married pagan wives and sold his birthright, with apparently no sense of responsibility for the call on this family to be God's blessing to the earth (25:31-34; 26:34-35). In a culture where the husband's will was law and Isaac was blind to God's choice, Rebekah took the only route she knew to secure God's promise.

Genesis is full of accounts that underline for Israel the miracle of their blessing and existence--three barren matriarchs (18:11; 25:21; 30:22), royal abduction or threatening of matriarchs (12:13; 20:2; Isaac repeated his father's example--26:7), and so on. Elsewhere in Genesis someone other than the patriarch makes a choice, nevertheless leaving the right land to the patriarch (13:9-13; 36:6-8). In the context of the themes the entire book emphasizes, it is consistent to believe that God worked through Rebekah's deception, as he worked through a variety of other means, to protect his chosen line.

This is not to say that the deception was God's preferred means to accomplish this, though he sometimes blessed deception when it would save human life from unjust oppressors (Ex 1:18-21; Josh 2:5-6; 1 Sam 16:1-3; 2 Sam 17:19-20; 2 Kings 8:10; Jer 38:24-27). As Jacob stole his brother's birthright through deception, so he is deceived through two sisters. When

Isaac asked Jacob his name, he lied to get the blessing (Gen 27:18-19), hence incurring his brother's murderous anger (27:41). His mother promised to send for him when it proved safe to return (27:45), but apparently she died in the meantime hence could not send for him, so when he is returning he expects that Esau still desires to kill him (32:11). Thus he struggles all night with the Lord or his agent, and he is confronted with his past. This time, before he can receive the blessing from God, he is asked his name and must tell the truth (32:26-27; and then gets a new name--32:28), in contrast to the time he sought his father's blessing (27:18-19). But God was with Jacob even in spite of himself; he met angels both going from (28:12) and returning to (32:2) the land. In this story, though Isaac outlives Rebekah, she was the one with the greater perception of God's purposes for their descendants.

15. Casting Lots in Acts 1:26

Some interpreters today suggest that the apostles made a mistake in casting lots for a twelfth apostle, even though it was before the day of Pentecost. The immediate context, however, suggests something positive; the believers were in prayerful unity (1:12-14; 2:1), and now Peter has exhorted them to replace the lost apostle (1:15-26). Would Luke spend so much space to describe a practice he disagreed with, and then fail to offer any word of correction?

Whole-book context in Acts actually invites us to read Luke and Acts together, for they were two volumes of one work (Acts 1:1-2; cf. Lk 1:1-4). When we read them together we see that Luke's Gospel also opens with a casting of lots, in this case, one used to select which priest would serve in the temple (Lk 1:9). In that case, God certainly controlled the lot, for by it Zechariah was chosen to serve in the temple, and subsequently received a divine promise specifically designed for himself and Elizabeth, the promise of a son, John the Baptist (1:13). If God controlled the lot in the opening story of volume one, why not in the opening story (after repeating the ascension) in volume 2? The background would help us further: if God controlled the lot throughout the Old Testament, including for selection of levitical ministries, why should we doubt that he used this method on this one occasion in Acts, before the Spirit's special guidance inaugurated with Pentecost (2:17).

16. Some Closing Observations on "Biblical Theology"

Sometimes today we start with specific doctrinal assumptions and read them into the Bible. The danger with this method is that it keeps us from ever learning anything new--if we read the Bible only as a textbook of what we already believe, we are likely to miss anything it has to teach and correct us. Thus it is important to learn the Bible's perspectives as they are written.

But while we affirm that the Bible is correct and does not contradict itself, we recognize that some books of the Bible emphasize some themes more than other books do. Thus, for example, if one reads the Book of Revelation, one is more likely to find an emphasis on Jesus' second coming than in the Gospel of John; in the Gospel of John, there is a heavier emphasis on eternal life available in the present. In the same way, when Paul writes to the Corinthians about speaking in tongues, he emphasizes its use as prayer; when Luke describes tongues in Acts, it functions as a demonstration that God transcends all linguistic barriers, fitting Luke's theme that the Spirit empowers God's people to cross cultural barriers. Different writers and books often have different emphases; these differences do noy contradict one another, but we must study them respectfully on their own terms before we try to put them together.

This principle is important in whole-book (or sometimes whole-author) context. When a specific passage seems obscure to us and we cannot tell which way the author meant it, it helps to look at the rest of the book to see what the author emphasizes. Thus, for example, the fact that the Gospel of John so often stresses that future hopes like "eternal life" are present realities (e.g., Jn 3:16, 36; 5:24-25; 11:24-26) may help shed light on how we approach John 14:2-3, as noted above. At the same time, we should never forget that each New Testament writing, however distinctive, is also part of a larger context of the teaching of apostolic Christianity, which had some common features. Thus, though the Gospel of John emphasizes the presence of the future, it in no way minimizes the fact that Jesus will return someday future as well (5:28-29; 6:39-40).

Whole book interpretation principles:

Before we close this chapter, we should summarize some whole book interpretation principles. Most of the chapter has been illustrating these principles.

- We must be careful never to "miss the forest for the trees," as the saying goes: We must not focus so much on difficult details at the beginning that we miss the larger picture of what the book of the Bible is trying to say. (One can work on more details later.)
- We should look for the themes that follow through any particular book in the Bible.
- We should get the flow of argument in any book of the Bible where that is relevant.
- It is often helpful to trace various themes where they occur in a book of the Bible, taking notes on them, or outline the flow of argument.

Chapter 4
Other Context Principles

We should briefly survey some other context principles: context of author; anticontext methods to avoid; and the value of outlining Scripture to catch the flow of thought.

Context of Author

In some cases, we have additional help in understanding a passage or statement in the Bible because we can look elsewhere at the particular author's style. Paul says that God inspired the Scriptures "through" people (Rom 1:2), which suggests that the author's point corresponds with God's point. It is therefore important to understand the author's point. Understanding inspiration recognizes that God inspired different writers in their own basic styles. Jeremiah and Isaiah and Ezekiel all heard God's message, but each has a very different style. God even gives Ezekiel a special nickname, "son of man."

Sometimes the author's style is relevant within the book. For example, when some people today claim that "abundant life" in John 10:10 refers to material prosperity, we should note that this is not what John means by "life" anywhere else (1:4; 3:15-16, 36; 4:14, 35; 5:24, 26, 29, 39-40; 6:27; etc.) If this were not enough, however, one could also note references to "life" by the same author in 1 John (1:1-2; 2:25; 3:14-15; 5:11-13, 16, 20). Some argue that Jesus healed everyone on the basis of Matthew 4:23. But does "all" mean every individual in the whole region? Matthew also says that they brought him "all" the sick in the whole province of Syria (which included Galilee and Judea); if he meant that literally, no one would have needed healing after this point (against the testimony of Acts and even the rest of Matthew's Gospel). Jesus did not heal everyone who was sick near him (13:58), although there were reasons for this and the text indicates that Jesus normally healed people. When we read Isaiah and the Psalms, "salvation" has a broader meaning than it usually bears in the New Testament, and we should respect the context of Isaiah's and the psalmists' usage and not read other texts into these.

Let me take two examples from Paul's writings. In neither case are we addressing a particular doctrine; a doctrine often may be based on other texts. But it is helpful to pick examples that will underline the point. For example, some say that the Church will not go through the Great Tribulation at the end of the age because Paul declares that we will not experience God's "wrath" (1 Thess 1:10; 5:9). This, however, is a questionable argument for that position. Occasionally Paul speaks of God's "wrath" in the present era (Rom 1:18), but usually when he uses the term he speaks of future wrath on the day of God's judgment (Rom 2:5, 8; 5:9; 9:22)--nowhere of the Great Tribulation before that day. Some interpreters want to appeal to the use of "wrath" in Revelation, but Revelation had not yet been written, so Paul could not expect the Thessalonians to simply flip over to Revelation to guess what he meant by "wrath." (If one does appeal to Revelation, however, this particular Greek word for "wrath" always refers to judgment at the end of the tribulation; the word which sometimes--not always--refers to the tribulation as God's anger is not even the same word!)

My second example from Paul is the trumpet in 1 Thessalonians 4:16 and 1 Corinthians 15:52; the latter text calls it the "last trumpet," so some interpreters want to parallel it with the seventh trumpet in Revelation. But again, Paul's original audience had no access to a book that had not been written yet. They could not simply flip over to Revelation to understand what Paul meant by the trumpet. They could not even flip from 1 Thessalonians to 1 Corinthians, since most of the first audience in Thessalonica would not have a copy of 1 Corinthians. (The early Christians probably had heard Paul share Jesus' teachings with them, and may have known about the trumpet later recorded in Matthew 24:31. In this sense, we can use Jesus' teachings as "background" for Paul's message. But jumping carelessly from one author to another, say from Paul to Revelation, can often yield inaccurate results.)

Most of our letters of Paul are relatively short. By contrast, many of his congregations knew him and were familiar with some points he was making; it is therefore helpful for us to get to know him better by familiarizing ourselves with all his extant writings. This helps us whenever we approach any particular writing of Paul's.

AntiContext methods to avoid

One must be very careful with word-studies, and should entirely avoid the usual sort of word-study sermons: These are equivalent to preaching from a dictionary rather than from the Bible! Thus some ministers preach on the different "kinds" of love in different passages, *agapao* love versus *phileo* love. But the distinction between these two "kinds" of love had virtually disappeared by the New Testament period, so they are often (probably even usually) used interchangeably! Tracing all the uses of a particular word in the Bible is helpful for finding out the different ways that word can be used. It should never form a sermon outline, however (the exception might be some passages in Proverbs), because that is preaching from a concordance rather than from a text studied in its context.

One should also avoid determining the meaning of words by their etymologies. That is, you cannot break a word down into its component parts and always come up with its meaning, and you usually cannot determine the meaning a word has by looking at how it was used centuries earlier or how the word originated. For a contemporary example, if one of my students called me a "nice professor," they might intend it as a compliment. But if I were committed to understanding words according to their origins, I could grow very angry. In English, "nice" is a friendly term; but its Latin source means "ignorant" or "foolish." So I could misunderstand someone calling me "nice" as that person calling me "ignorant"! We know that English does not work that way, and we should not expect ancient languages to work that way, either.

For example, some take the Greek word for "repent," *metanoieo*, and divide it into two parts, of which the second, *noieo*, is related to thinking. Therefore, they say, "repent" simply means a change of mind. The problem with this interpretation is that the meaning of words is determined by their usage, not by their origins! The New Testament generally uses "repent" not in the Greek sense of "changing one's mind" but in the sense of "turn" in the Old Testament prophets: a radical turning of our lives from sin to God's righteousness.

Another example of this problem occurs when interpreters speak of the Church as the "called-out ones" based on the Greek word for church, *ekklesia*. We are, to be sure, "called-out," but we know that for other reasons, not because we can determine that from *ekklesia*. Some divide *ekklesia* into *ek*, meaning "out of," and *kaleo*, which means "call." But *ekklesia* had already been used by Greeks for centuries to mean an "assembly" or "gathering"; Jewish people who knew Greek spoke of the congregation of Israel in the wilderness as God's *ekklesia*. So the New Testament does not make up a new word to call Christians the "called-out-ones"; rather, it uses a standard term for an assembly, and probably the first Christians thought especially of God's own assembly in the Old Testament, his people.

People can twist Greek the way they can twist English, Hausa, or anything else. When Jehovah's Witnesses claim that John 1:1 calls Jesus "a God" because there is no definite article ("the") in front of "God" there, they neglect several factors, of which I will briefly summarize two. First, "God" does not always have a definite article in John's Gospel; the God who sent John the Baptist does not have a definite article (Jn 1:6), but Jehovah's Witnesses never say he was simply "a god." Second, grammatically "God" is a predicate nominative in "the Word was God," and predicate nominatives usually omit definite articles. Even without moving any further, we can see that the Jehovah's Witness interpretation here is based on a lack of knowledge of Greek.

Some people speak of *zoe* as the "God-kind-of-life," but *zoe* refers to human life just as easily. Some misinterpret Greek grammar, claiming that "faith of God" must mean "the God-kind-of-faith"; it could mean that, but in context probably means "faith in God." Some claim that "now" in Hebrews 11:1 means present-tense "now"; but the Greek term there means "but" or "and." Someone once claimed to me that Christians would all become Christ, because he would come with "ten-thousands of himself" in Jude 14. The person's error was simple--"ten-thousands of him" is the appropriate way to say in Greek, "ten-thousands belonging to him"--but it led them into a serious doctrinal error. More often than not (there may be some exceptions), when someone comes up with an interpretation based on Greek or Hebrew that contradicts what one would have thought from reading the rest of the Bible, they may be reading into the Greek or the Hebrew something that is not there. It is helpful to learn Greek and Hebrew for yourself, but if you cannot, sticking with a couple good translations is usually safe.

The most common anticontext method is practiced by cults like Jehovah's Witnesses by also widespread in churches of most denominations. We read into the text what we already expect to find there, because of our doctrine or because of how we have heard a story told! How often have we read a Bible story only to realize that part of the story we always heard is not in that passage? How often have we read our doctrine (maybe even a correct doctrine, supported by other texts) into a text or texts that did not really address the issue? When this happens, Christians from different groups can no longer use the Bible as a common basis for seeking truth, because we are all "sure" of our own interpretations, which we sometimes cannot defend from context! It is important enough to respect the Bible enough to let it speak for itself. If our doctrine is not in a passage, we do not need to read it in; our doctrine is probably in some other passage--or else respect for the Bible's authority may require us to fix our doctrine. In this way we are open to fresh discoveries in the Bible each time we study it. At the same time, this does not mean that we throw away everything we have already learned and start with nothing each day. We build on what we have already learned, and go back and change particular interpretations only as we study the text as honestly as possible and find a need to change. This way we can also dialogue with other honest Christians around the Scriptures.

Outlining to Get the Flow of Context

Outlining a passage's or a book's structure can often help a person follow the flow of thought. Some texts break down easily into an obvious structure. For example:

1. Ephesians 5:21-6:9
5:21 (thesis statement): Submitting to one another in the fear of Christ
    1. 5:22-33: Wives and husbands
    2. 6:1-4: Children and fathers
    3. 6:5-9: Slaves and slaveholders
2. Matthew 5:21-48
    1. Angry enough to kill (5:21-26)
    2. Coveting others sexually (5:27-30)
    3. Unfaithfulness by divorce (5:31-32)
    4. Integrity better than oaths (5:33-37)
    5. Avoiding resistance (5:38-42)
    6. Loving your enemy (5:43-47)
    Conclusion: Be perfect like God (5:48)
3. Matthew 6:1-18
Thesis statement: 6:1: Do righteousness only for God to see, or you lose your reward with him.
    1. Do charity secretly (6:2-4)
    2. Pray secretly (6:5-15)
        a. Instructions for prayer (6:5-8)
        b. Sample prayer (6:9-13)
        c. Elaboration on forgiveness (6:14-15)
    3. Fast secretly (6:16-18)

One could also subdivide 6:5-13 as follows:

A   Don't pray like (hypocrites, 6:5)
    B   Pray like this (secretly, 6:6)
A'   Don't pray like (pagans, 6:7-8)
    B'   Pray like this (Lord's prayer, 6:9-13)

4. Psalm 150

1. Where to praise God (everywhere, 150:1)
2. What to praise God for (his works and character, 150:2)
3. How to praise God (with all available instruments, 150:3-5)
4. Who should praise God (everyone, 150:6)

5. Psalm 1

1. The way and blessing of the righteous (1:1-3)
   a. They do not enjoy sinful company (1:1)
   b. They think on God's law (1:2)
   c. God will bless them with success (1:3)
2. The way and judgment of the wicked (1:4-5)
   a. The wicked will face judgment (1:4)
   b. The wicked will not enjoy righteous company (1:5)
3. Summary

Not all outlines come so simply, however; some outlines of thought may be more complicated. Thus, for example, one can divide Romans 1:18-32 into a simple outline: God judges the world for preferring idols to his truth (1:18-23); they fall into sexual sin (1:24-27); and ultimately every kind of sin (1:28-32). But a more detailed outline might also reveal Paul's line of thought in more detail (I adapt the NASB below):

> Rom. 1:10 always in my prayers making request, if perhaps now at last by the will of God I may succeed in coming to you.

> [why?--reason for 1:10]

Rom. 1:11 For

> I long to see you in order that I may impart some spiritual gift to you, that you may be established;
>   [=]
> Rom. 1:12 that is,
> that I may be encouraged together with you while among you, each of us by the other's faith, both yours and mine.

> Rom. 1:13 And I do not want you to be unaware, brethren, that often I have planned to come to you (and have been prevented thus far)

> [why? *purpose* for planning to come]
> **in order that**

> I might obtain some fruit among you also, even as among the rest of the Gentiles.

> **[grammatically new point (though logically continues explanation for what precedes]**

Rom 1:14 I am under obligation both to Greeks and to barbarians, both to the wise and to the foolish.

[1:14 provides the reason for 1:15]
Rom. 1:15 Thus,

for my part, I am eager to preach the gospel to you also who are in Rome.

[1:16a also provides the reason for 1:15]
Rom. 1:16 For
I am not ashamed of the gospel,

[1:16b provides the reason for 1:16a]
for

it is the power of God for salvation to everyone who believes, to the Jew first and also to the Greek.

[Why is it God's salvific power for both Jew and Greek? 1:17 provides the reason for 1:16b (both Jew and Gentile come to God on equal terms through faith)
Rom. 1:17 For

in it the righteousness of God is revealed from faith to faith;
[basis for knowing this:]

as it is written, "But the righteous person shall live by faith."

[Why must the righteous come by faith? 1:17 is predicated on the entire section that follows in 1:18-2:29 and beyond--all are equally *lost*]
1:18 For

the wrath of God is revealed from heaven against all ungodliness and unrighteousness of people=who suppress the truth in unrighteousness,

[why is God so angry? wrath (v. 18) *because* they should've known better (v. 19)]
Rom. 1:19 because

that which is known about God is evident within them;

[why?]
for
God made it evident to them.

[how?]
Rom. 1:20 For

since the creation of the world His invisible attributes, His eternal power and divine nature,

132

have been clearly seen, being understood through what has been made

[with the result that--the closing line shows the result of the preceding one]
so that
they are without excuse.

[why? basis for the result in the last line of 1:20, hence rehearsing the reason of the earlier lines of 1:20]
Rom. 1:21-23 For even though they knew God, they did not honor Him as God, or give thanks; but they became futile in their speculations, and their foolish heart was darkened. Professing to be wise, they became fools, and exchanged the glory of the incorruptible God for an image in the form of corruptible man and of birds and four-footed animals and crawling creatures.

[1:24 happens *because* of 1:23--sexual sin (perverting God's image in humanity) stems from idolatry (perverting God's image directly)]
Rom. 1:24 Therefore
God gave them over in the lusts of their hearts to impurity, that their bodies might be dishonored among them.

[1:25 is the basis for 1:24--rehearses the thought of 1:21-23]

<u>Rom. 1:25 For</u>
they exchanged the truth of God for a lie, and worshiped and served the creature rather than the Creator, who is blessed forever. Amen.

[1:26 happens *because* of 1:25, and rehearses and develops the thought of 1:24]
<u>Rom. 1:26-28 For</u>
this reason God gave them over to degrading passions; for their women exchanged the natural function for that which is unnatural, and in the same way also the men abandoned the natural function of the woman and burned in their desire toward one another, men with men committing indecent acts and receiving in their own persons the due penalty of their error. And just as they did not see fit to acknowledge God any longer, God gave them over to a depraved mind, to do those things which are not proper, {followed by vice list}

Outlining passages can prove very useful in seeking to convey biblical truths. Larger outlines of passages often can provide the main points for a sermon or an outline for an inductive Bible study. In this case the structure of the text becomes the structure of your sermon--making you depend still more on the Bible for what you will teach! One can also list various lessons in a passage and make them one's main points; or one can simply tell the story in the text, and mention the lessons as they arise.

More important than the specific outline in many cases is noting recurrent themes in the text and how they connect with each other and with the context. In any case, we discipline ourselves and our hearers to understand the Bible better when we treat it passage by passage rather than skipping indiscriminately from one to another.

Chapter 5
Bible Background

In any communication, some matters are stated but others can be left assumed. For instance, I am writing in English, on the assumption that I and my readers both know English; if Paul wrote to the Corinthians in Greek, he could assume that they knew Greek. I assume that my readers know what a Bible is, and would be safe to assume that my readers know what a car is, what a radio is, and what pounded yam is (though Paul's readers knew none of these things, except what the Old Testament part of the Bible was). Paul could likewise allude to specific customs his readers practiced without explaining them, because the Corinthians already knew exactly what he meant (e.g., "baptism for the dead," 1 Cor 15:29). But for us to understand Paul's meaning we must either know Greek or have a translation, and we must either know the culture the biblical writers shared with their audiences or have access to resources that help explain that culture. What the writer could *assume* as part of his meaning was as much a part of the meaning as what he had to state.

We have noted above the importance of whole-book context, because most books of the Bible stress particular themes addressing particular issues. We should not skip from one book of the Bible to another (except where one book specifically refers back to an earlier and widely circulated one), at least not until we have figured out each passage in its own context first. But one reason particular books emphasize particular themes is that they addressed particular situations. Although people sometimes ignore such verses, many verses explicitly state particular audiences for these books--for instance, the Christians in Rome (Rom 1:7) or in Corinth (1 Cor 1:2). There are appropriate ways to apply these books to today, but first we must take seriously what these works explicitly claim to be: works addressed to specific audiences in specific times and places. In other words, before we can determine how to apply the ancient meaning today, we must understand the ancient meaning. To skip this important step in Bible interpretation is to ignore what the Bible claims for itself.

When Paul wrote letters, the very genre in which he wrote reminds us that he addressed specific situations, as letters usually do. Thus, for example, in 1 Corinthians Paul addresses questions about food offered to idols, head coverings, and other issues that Christians today usually view as relevant only in some cultures. The letter also addresses division between followers of Paul and followers of Apollos, which does not occur in exactly that form anywhere today; we have to deal with division in the church, but few people today claim to follow Apollos. If we read letters as letters, we remember to look for the specific situations they address.

We should consider the relevance even of narratives to the first audience they addressed. For instance, if Moses wrote Genesis to those who had just been released from slavery in Egypt, they could have identified readily with Joseph, who had also been a slave in Egypt before his exaltation. The repeated emphasis on the promise of the holy land in Genesis also would provide great encouragement for Israelites about ready to go in and conquer it. Considering such relevance of the Bible to its original hearers does not make the Bible any less relevant for us; rather, it teaches us how to discover its relevance properly. Everything in the Bible is for all time, but not everything in the Bible is for all circumstances.

Some examples of culture-specific teachings in the Bible

We all recognize that some commands in the Bible were limited to the period that they address. Moses says to build a "fence" around the roof lest you incur bloodguilt if anyone falls from it (Deut 22:8), yet most of us today do not build fences around our roofs. Are we disobeying this passage? But back in Moses' day, people had flat roofs (like homes near Kano); and in Moses' day, people would spend time on the roof, often with their neighbors. Yet if a neighbor child fell off the roof, she could get hurt. So Moses commands us to build a parapet around the roof to protect our neighbor. Today, if we do not take neighbors on the roof, the point for us is not the parapet; the principle is watching out for our neighbor's safety (for instance, making someone riding with us wear a seat belt). But we would not have discovered the principle if we had not understood the background.

Some today seek to get doctrine especially from Paul's letters, so let us take some New Testament letters as examples. Paul tells Timothy to go to Troas and bring his cloak from there (2 Tim 4:13), yet none of us tries to obey this explicit command of Scripture by going to the excavations at Troas and looking for Paul's cloak. (Even though Paul also calls Titus to come to him in Tit 3:12, we do not view visiting Paul in Rome as a command to us today.) Even if Timothy did not get the cloak, and even if it still exists, and even if we could be sure it was Paul's, only one person could actually retrieve the cloak. And none of us could then take it to Paul! This passage of Scripture is addressed to the only person who could fulfill it, namely Timothy. Likewise, do we really need to beware of Alexander the coppersmith (2 Tim 4:14-15)? Given the mortality rate for people over 150 years old, he has surely been dead for a long time. (For some other situation-specific allusions, see e.g., 2 Tim 1:2-6; 3:14-15; 4:20; Tit 1:4-5.) We can learn *principles* from Paul's bond with Timothy and his warnings against opposition, but we cannot press these statements literally as *commands* for today.

We recognize these as absurd examples; "Those were commands given only to Timothy!" we protest. Our protest is correct, but how many other commands in 1 and 2 Timothy may have been only for Timothy or only for first-century Ephesian culture? We cannot settle that question by simply guessing at an answer we might prefer; nor can we ignore the question and hope to be consistent. Paul was probably aware that the Spirit was guiding him as he wrote (1 Cor 7:40; 14:37), but it is quite doubtful that he expected Christians to be trying to apply this letter directly and only to themselves two thousand years later--or even that human history would continue for two thousand more years (cf. 1 Cor 7:29; "we" in 1 Thess 4:17). If they did try to apply his letter to Timothy, he would expect them to take into account what this piece of Scripture explicitly claims to be: a *letter to Timothy* (1 Tim 1:2; 2 Tim 1:2).

Many Christians today question the faith of others who do not interpret literally every text that we interpret literally; yet all of us refuse to take some texts literally--or at least we refuse to apply some texts directly to ourselves without taking into account that our situation is different. Paul tells Timothy to avoid water and take some wine for his stomach's sake (1 Tim 5:23). Paul is certainly not telling Timothy to get drunk; in Paul's day, most wine was watered down two parts water to every part wine, and wine was not distilled, so the alcohol content was not high. At the same time, before refrigeration and hermetic sealing, any grape juice that had been kept for some months after the last grape vintage included some alcohol content. Would we tell every Christian today with a stomach ache to avoid water and go have a watered-down beer? Or was that simply the best remedy available in Paul's day, in contrast to our own?

In fact, *all* Scripture is universally applicable (2 Tim 3:16). This does not mean, however, that it is not articulated in culture-specific and language-specific ways. Rather, it means that we have to take the situation into account when we interpret Scripture, reading it like case studies applying to specific situations to find its principles which we can then apply in other situations. Otherwise one would end up like some western missionaries who mixed up their own culture with the biblical message and then told African Christians they had to keep both the Bible and western culture to be good Christians (which resembles what Paul's opponents did in Galatia--Gal 2:3-5; 6:12-13).

Inspiration does not change a writing's *genre*, or type of literature. Psalms are still psalms, narrative is still narrative, and epistles are still epistles. (We will deal with genre in a subsequent chapter.) Pastoral letters, like sermons addressed to local congregations, can contain universal and culture-specific exhortations side-by-side; this is true in inspired, biblical letters just as it is true in other letters.

For example, I sometimes write letters of exhortation containing mainly universal principles relevant to the particular situation I am adressing. Yet in those same letters I may include some exhortations relevant only to the situation I am addressing. Unless I consciously write expecting other, future readers *outside* the situation, I may never stop to distinguish my universal and situation-specific exhortations. Because I intend all my exhortations to be relevant to my immediate audience I do not write these two kinds of exhortations in different ways or express them in different literary forms.

A later reader might therefore distinguish which I thought was which only by reconstructing the situation and comparing my other writings addressing specific situations. Thus murmuring is always wrong (1 Cor 10:10; Phil 2:14); eating idol-food is sometimes wrong (1 Cor 8-10); women's authority as ministers of the word was sometimes limited but sometimes commended (cf. Rom 16:1-12; Phil 4:3).

Paul provides many direct commands that we do not observe today, and some that we cannot observe today. How many Christians put money into savings the first day of every week for a collection for the saints in Jerusalem (1 Cor 16:1-3)? Paul commands his readers to receive Epaphroditus (Phil 2:29), but since the latter is now dead, we cannot fulfill this command literally. Paul exhorts his readers to pray for the ministry of himself and his companions (2 Thess 3:1-2), but it is too late to pray for their ministry today. Instead we learn more general principles about hospitably receiving and praying for God's servants.

Must a transcultural application be absurd before we will limit it? Or do these "absurd" examples point out to us the way we ought to read Paul's letters consistently? To claim that only the *obviously* culturally limited passages are in fact culturally limited is simply to beg the question of interpretation methods. If these examples remind us of the *genre* in which Paul writes, they remind us that Paul could freely mix directly transcultural statements with those that addressed merely specific situations. It should not surprise us that Paul relates to his readers where they are at; he specifically states that this is his missionary strategy (1 Cor 9:19-23; 10:31-33), and most of us today similarly try to be relevant to those to whom we speak.

When Paul exhorts men to pray properly (1 Tim 2:8), shall we assume that women should not pray properly? Or shall we assume that, just as Paul had a specific situation to address with the women in that congregation (2:9-15), he also had a specific problem in mind addressing the local men's behavior (2:8)? Given other passages which commend (Rom 16:1-12; cf. Judg 4:4; Acts 2:17-18; 21:9; Phil 4:2-3) or permit (1 Cor 11:4-5) various ministries of women, is it possible that the limitations of 1 Tim 2:11-12 address a special situation? The answers to some of these questions are much debated, but our desire to be consistent in the way we interpret the Bible may invite us to ask such questions.

The office of an "overseer" (1 Tim 3:1), like most other local-church offices in the New Testament, arose in a specific cultural context; it was practical for the church to borrow models of leadership from the synagogues that already worked in the Roman world. Is it possible that modern denominations' arguments about forms of church leadership may make too much of a matter that is not really central to Paul's point? Some would retain as transcultural the requirement that one rule one's family properly as a condition for ruling the church (3:4-5). But this borrows ancient Mediterranean requirements for respectable leadership, in a culture where paternal authority could be enforced by severe discipline (in theory even execution)--a culture which differs markedly from our own. Granted, some regard these models of church order as transcultural, so we should turn to other, more clearly culture-specific examples.

Perhaps more significant are passages providing instructions not merely to Timothy but to the church as a whole. How many would regard as transcultural the warning that widows younger than sixty will spread bad talk (probably best translated "false teaching"; 1 Tim 5:11-13), or that fables circulate especially among older women (4:7)? Here, for example, widows must not be put on the roll for church support unless they are at least sixty years old, have been married only once (5:9), have raised children and washed strangers' feet (5:10), and also have no extended family to care for them (5:8). Americans usually relegate to government programs the caring for widows; Africans, much closer to the biblical culture, normally support them through the extended family. But in most cultures, so few widows today have washed strangers' feet that our churches can claim to obey Paul's teaching without supporting them anyway! Paul commands that younger widows must remarry, not taking the pledge of membership in the order of older widows supported by the church (5:11, 14). But how they can obey this precept if they do not find husbands is not quite clear. In Paul's day there was a shortage of women (possibly due to the pagan practice of female child abandonment), and most women therefore sought and found husbands quickly. In many black American churches, however, single women outnumber single men more than two to one; in parts of rural India and China, by contrast, men far outnumber women.

Paul is clear that some of his commands in the Pastoral Epistles relate to avoiding apostasy (1 Tim 5:15) and--a matter related to the views of the broader culture--public reproach (1 Tim 3:2, 6-7, 10; 6:1; Tit 1:6-7; 2:5, 8, 10). This includes his exhortations concerning the obedience of slaves (1 Tim 6:1-2; cf. Tit 2:9-10), which most Christians today would grant addressed a specific cultural situation. If the principles are more binding than the situation-specific exhortations that illustrate them, we may wish to consider how today's situation differs from that of the first century, and what practices support or hinder the Church's witness.

But none of this means that these passages have nothing to teach us. Paul specifically writes to Timothy, Titus, or to particular churches, but we can learn from his inspired wisdom for their situations as long as we pause to think how it might translate differently into our somewhat different situations. Human nature and God's nature have not changed, and we can take into account the changes in culture as long as we know something about the original cultures of the Bible. For example, Paul specifically left Timothy in Ephesus to warn against those teaching false doctrines (1 Tim 1:3), and exhorts Timothy to do so according to the prophecies given him (1:18; 4:14; cf. 2 Tim 1:6); he also addresses specific false teachers (1:20), who are now dead. Although Paul did not leave us in Ephesus nor did we receive Timothy's prophecies, there are plenty of transcultural principles here, such as fighting dangerous doctrines, or heeding words of wisdom or properly tested prophecy. But again, noting that specific exhortations can have more general relevance does not allow us to simply assume that we *know* that transcultural relevance before we have studied the situation carefully.

When Paul tells Timothy to drink a little wine for his stomach's sake (1 Tim 5:23), we learn that it is sometimes necessary to take medicine. God often heals instantly in answer to prayer, but at many other times he has provided us natural means by which to improve our health. (By "natural" we mean what he has created in nature, not occult practices which involve evil spirits.) Yet recognizing that this is the only way we can apply some Scriptures must summon us to consistency: perhaps this is the way all Scripture is to be read to be profitable for teaching (2 Tim 3:16).

This is how Paul often read the Old Testament: Those events were written down as examples for us, both positive and negative (1 Cor 10:6, 11). In the same way, we should read the stories in the Bible as case studies--as examples how God dealt with people in particular kinds of situations. Then we can take warning or encouragement when we recognize analogous situations today! But we must make sure the situations are really analogous. That is, God destroyed the disobedient in the wilderness (1 Cor 10:6-10); that does not mean that *obedient* people should fear destruction! We do not simply apply *directly to ourselves* every passage we read without taking into account the difference in situation.

The same is true for Paul's letters. Paul addressed specific situations in a specific culture. We cannot simply apply his words to all cultures directly, as if we can ignore differences. When Paul says to "Greet one another with a holy kiss" (Rom 16:16; 1 Cor 16:20; 2 Cor 13:12; 1 Thess 5:26), he uses the standard form of intimate greeting in his culture. (Familial kisses were often light kisses on the lips.) Today Christians should still greet one another affectionately, but in most of our cultures few of us actually use kisses to do it, especially the kinds of kisses used back then. Although Christian interpreters today differ as to where to draw the line, *no* one tries to fulfill literally every command of the Bible with no account for the difference in situation. No one tries to get Paul's cloak at Troas and bring it to him.

Using Cultural Background

But merely pointing out that we must take into account culture in Bible interpretation does not tell us precisely how to use it. For this, we must follow several steps.

1. Obtaining the Correct Background

We must first take into account, as best as possible, the specific culture and situations the original writers of the Bible addressed. For instance, knowing about the use of kisses in greetings in Paul's culture is helpful. If we are going to practice (or not practice) head coverings today, we should know what head coverings looked like in Paul's day (hence what he meant by them) and why he supported their use (to see if we share those reasons).

Where do we get this background? Some of the background is often in the Bible itself. For instance, we can learn much about the times in which Isaiah prophesied by reading the accounts of the kings in whose reigns he prophesied (listed in Is 1:1) in 2 Kings; likewise about the situations Jeremiah addressed roughly a century later. Acts 17:1-9 tells us about the founding of the church in Thessalonica, which in turn gives us some background for 1 and 2 Thessalonians. We can also reconstruct some of the specific situation addressed based on what the texts themselves emphasize. For instance, Paul seems to address Jewish-Gentile division in Rome, conflicts between the wealthier and less wealthy Christians in Corinth, and so forth. Noticing these patterns in these letters can help us reconstruct what sorts of issues the writers had to contend with, shedding light on many details in the letters.

But not all the background is available in the Bible itself. When Paul wrote to the Corinthians, he did not provide a translation of his letter into Hausa, Ibo, English or Arabic; later translators provide that for us, but Paul wrote his letter in Greek, because that was the language most or all of the Corinthian Christians spoke. In the same way, he does not pause to explain customs or situations that he and the Corinthians both knew; they are *assumed* in his meaning, but modern readers need to do some research to find out what he meant. Paul would welcome later readers to learn from his letters, but he could not write a letter that would address all languages and cultures at once; he would expect us to learn his language and culture or use tools that provide it.

More specific knowledge of the culture requires more work, because not everyone possesses biblical background resources outside the Bible. On some issues (like holy kisses, Jewish burial customs or waterpots in Cana) we recognize that the Bible's culture often differs from our own. But often even when we think we can take for granted that our own cultural background (as if all modern Christians shared the same culture!) qualifies us to understand the Bible, we are mistaken. Many of us miss the shock that would have greeted the first hearers of Jesus' parable of the prodigal son: no respectable father would have divided his inheritance at a son's demand, run to greet his son, or welcomed him home safe without punishment.

Jesus compares God to an indulgent, overly lenient father--showing just how merciful he has been in view of our rebellion against him.

Often we miss the point of the passage because we are unfamiliar with the culture in which it was written. Some cultures, such as Middle Eastern and Mediterranean cultures or some traditional rural African culture, are closer to the cultures in the Old and New Testament than most western cultures are. (Bedouin culture may be closest to that necessary for understanding Abraham; a mixture of peasant farmers and Jewish sages gives us the best background for Mark; Paul's writings reflect a broader cosmopolitan, urban Greco-Roman world.) But none of us dare assume that we will always interpret the Bible correctly without consulting the ancient culture. African cultures are closer to biblical cultures than western cultures are, but this makes it easy to miss the fact that sometimes African and biblical cultures differ (for example, in Corinth either husband or wife could divorce the other regardless of the other's protests--1 Cor 7:15).

Various sources provide information on ancient Mediterranean cultures. Someone who wants to study the Gospels in detail, for instance, should read in addition to the Old Testament the Apocrypha (a section contained in Catholic but not Protestant Bibles), especially Wisdom of Solomon and Sirach; some of the Dead Sea Scrolls (especially the Manual of Discipline and War Scroll) and so-called Pseudepigrapha (especially 1 Enoch; Epistle of Aristeas; 4 Ezra and 2 Baruch); parts of Josephus (especially his *Life, Against Apion*, and parts of the *War*); and probably the tractate Aboth in the Mishnah. Because most students do not have access to all these resources, one might use a Bible encyclopedia (like the new *International Standard Bible Encyclopedia*) to get answers for specific questions one has. But sometimes one does not even know which questions one should ask without knowing some of the background.

For that reason, one of the simplest and most available beginning tools is the *IVP Bible Background Commentary*. The New Testament portion provides background on each passage or verse of the New Testament. Years ago I wanted such a tool, but because none was available, spent many years researching ancient Mediterranean culture to provide it in one volume, passage-by-passage, to make it widely available to all Bible readers. Since that time other background commentaries have also been produced. *The IVP Bible Background Commentary* provides a bibliography of sources useful for further research into ancient Mediterranean culture, for those who are able to pursue it further.

2. Determine How the Passage Relates to its Culture

We should know the culture and situation well enough to understand why the biblical writers addressed what they addressed the way they did. Once we understand the culture and situation, we need to understand what the writers say to the situation. In the passage you are studying, does the author agree with the views of his culture on this matter? For instance, when Jesus tells his disciples to offer private reproof before public rebuke (Matt 18:15-17), he is in agreement with the usual Jewish way of doing things in his day. In some other cases, biblical writers may adopt neutral aspects of the cultures they are addressing for the sake of being a relevant witness within those cultures, as Paul clearly explains that he does in 1 Corinthians 9:19-23.

Does a biblical writer disagree with some aspect of his culture? For instance, although the Israelites had some sacrifices the Canaanites had (like sin offerings), they did not have offerings to make it rain. Many pagans thought offerings to their gods could secure rain; but Israel's God promised to simply send rain if his people obeyed his covenant. Mesopotamian law required that any person who harbored an escaped slave should be executed; by contrast, God commanded Israelites to harbor escaped slaves (Deut 23:15).

Does the biblical writer modify a standard view of his culture, even while (often) communicating his message in culturally intelligible forms? This is one of the most frequent ways biblical writers related to their cultures. For instance, from Aristotle onward Greeks and Romans often emphasized that the male head of the household must rule his wife, children and slaves. But Paul, while taking over the topic, modifies the instructions: he tells a husband not how to rule his wife, but how to love her (Eph 5:25). The wife must submit, but as a form of Christian submission that all Christians must learn to practice (Eph 5:21-22). If we read this passage as if Paul were saying exactly the same thing as Aristotle, we would miss his point.

Likewise, God instructs the Israelites to build the tabernacle with a holy of holies, sanctuary and outer court just as in Egyptian temples, but this makes the contrast all the more striking: atop God's ark there is no image of the deity as in Egyptian temples. Sometimes biblical writers, for the sake of their witness, adopted aspects of their culture that were good or neutral; but this invites us to pay all the closer attention to where these writers contradict their culture.

3. Applying the Biblical Writers' Message

We cannot determine whether every culture or situation must address matters the same way the biblical writers did until we understand the biblical writers' reasons for making the particular arguments they do. But once we have a good idea about why the biblical writers addressed particular situations the way they did, we can begin to ask how they would have applied the same principles in very different situations.

For example, knowing why women wore head coverings in Paul's day helps us understand why he gives the instructions he does. Most women in the eastern Mediterranean world covered their hair in public as a sign of sexual modesty; thus the lower class women in the churches were concerned when some upper class women refused to wear them. (Hair constituted the primary object of male lust in the ancient Mediterranean world, so married women were required to keep their hair covered; some modern "head coverings" fail to do this.) Paul therefore addressed issues of ostentation, seductiveness, sexual modesty and class division in the church, all of which are transcultural issues.

But would Paul solve matters of sexual modesty or class division in the same way in every culture as he did in Corinth? Would the head covering provide a solution to such issues in every culture? Could head coverings in some cultures become signs of ostentation, showing off wealth? Could they in some cultures actually become tools of seduction the way jewels and costly array sometimes were in Paul's culture? What of a culture where only well-to-do people could afford to wear head coverings, thus introducing class division into the church? Is it possible that in churches in some parts of the world, *wearing* a had covering (as opposed to not wearing one) might draw attention to the wearer?

In such cases, do we follow Paul's specific example for his culture, or do we follow the transcultural principles Paul used to make a specific case for a specific culture? This is why it is so important for us to take into account cultural background and read Scripture consistently in light of it: If God inspired the writers to address their own culture in a particular way, how would they have addressed our culture today? Which are the principles and which are the specific examples that illustrated those principles in the situations the biblical writers addressed?

Jesus interpreted Scripture this way. The Pharisees were interested in detailed regulations, but Jesus was more interested in the principles (Matt 12:7). Jesus took into account the human *reasons* some Scriptures were given: some things God permitted because of the hardness of their hearts (Mk 10:5), but their real goal should be to understand God's ideal purposes (Mk 10:6-9). They cited a law; he cited a story. All Scripture is inspired and useful for teaching (2 Tim 3:16), so the issue is not that one kind of writing is more useful than another. The issue is that they saw only details, whereas Jesus looked for the *reasons* for the details. Jesus claimed that what mattered most was justice, mercy and faith (Matt 23:23)--the heart of God's word. Paul in the same way disagreed with his contemporaries on what was fundamental, arguing that it is God's own power that saves us, not secondary issues like circumcision or food laws. This method of interpretation requires us to keep central what matters most (the gospel and obedience to God's will), rather than becoming legalistic on secondary matters that could distract us from the heart of the gospel.

Much of the New Testament consists simply of examples how to relate the basic message of the gospel to various concrete historical situations and challenges. We must likewise learn how to relate the central message of Christ to our various situations today, never losing sight of what is the central principle and what are simply the cultural expressions. Many early missionaries came with a gospel contextualized for their own culture, say American or European versions of Christianity. Usually they remained largely faithful to the Bible, but they often failed to discern the difference between the Bible's actual teaching and the way they had applied it for the issues that confronted their particular cultures. Thus they sometimes forced African Christians to adopt western music styles, clothing styles, wedding ceremony styles, and so forth because they had assumed these customs to be Christian. Today we know better, and today we must avoid making the same mistake. We should be able to distinguish between the Bible's universal principles and how it applied those principles in the cultures it addressed. (Again, we affirm that all Scripture is God's message. But it was first God's message to the original cultures to which God sent it, so for us to hear it properly today we must take into account how God related it to those cultures.) Likewise, we must distinguish between what the Bible teaches for all cultures and how we have applied it specifically to the situations we must address.

Of course, if we are not careful, people can use culture to explain away things in the Bible; that is a danger we must strive hard to avoid. But people have been explaining away things in the Bible for centuries without using culture, so this danger should not make us afraid to use background in the appropriate manner. We simply need to use it conscientiously, diligent to find the truth. The only appropriate starting point for finding wisdom is the fear of the Lord (Prov 1:7); if we fear him we will be careful to truly understand his truth, wherever the evidence of the Bible genuinely leads us, rather than ways to explain that truth away.

Examples of Background

Here we provide only a few limited samples concerning the use of background; fuller details are available in the *IVP Bible Background Commentary:*

New Testament mentioned above. But first of all, some background is available in the Bible itself. This is especially true when biblical writers depend on what other biblical writers proclaimed before them; the prophets often depend on the law of Moses (though usually without quoting it); the New Testament regularly depends on the Old.

Two passages where the New Testament specifically assumes Old Testament background include John 1:14-18; 4:23-24. Ancient Near Eastern and northeast African background will be relevant for understanding the tabernacle, the Hagar story, and some other accounts in the Bible. Finally, Jewish and Greco-Roman sources will shed light on various New Testament passages. I include more New Testament examples only because that is my own area of specialization, not as if it were more important.

1. The New Word in John 1:14-18

Modern writers have proposed many valuable aspects of background for the "Word," but probably the most obvious is what the "Word" was in the Old Testament: God's word was the law, the Scripture he had given to Israel. John probably wrote his Gospel especially for Jewish Christians. Opponents of these Jewish Christians had probably kicked them out of their synagogues and claimed that they had strayed from God's Word in the Bible. Far from it, John replies:

Jesus is the epitome of all that God taught in Scripture, for Jesus himself is God's Word and revelation.

John probably alludes to one story in particular, the account of when Moses went up to receive the law the second time in Exodus 33 and 34. Israel had broken the covenant and God had judged them; now he gives Moses the law again but does not wish to "dwell" with Israel. Moses pleads with God to dwell with them, and then pleads with God to show him his glory. "No one can see my full glory," God told him, "but I will show you part of my glory, and make my goodness pass before you."

As God passed before Moses, Moses witnessed an astounding spectacle of glory; but especially God revealed his "goodness," his holy character, to Moses. As he passed before Moses, he described himself as "abounding in covenant love and covenant faithfulness," which could be translated, "full of grace and truth." And after God was finished revealing his character, Moses protested, "God, if that is the way you are, then please forgive us and dwell with us." And God promised to do so.

Some thirteen centuries later, the apostle John spoke of himself and his fellow eyewitnesses of Jesus in a manner like Moses. "We beheld Jesus' glory," he said, "full of grace and truth" (Jn 1:14). He builds to a climax in 1:17: "For the law was given through Moses, but grace and truth came through Jesus." To be sure, God revealed his grace and truth to Moses when he gave him the law; but Moses saw only *part* of God's glory, only part of his grace and truth. "No one has seen God at any time," John reminds us, alluding back to God's warning to Moses that he could not see all of God's glory; but now "the only God, who is in the Father's bosom, has revealed fully God's character" (1:18). Moses saw part of God's glory, but those who walked with Jesus saw all of God's glory, for to see him is to see the Father (Jn 14:7).

Whole book context explains the point here more fully. God's glory is revealed in various ways in Jesus (2:11; 11:4), but the ultimate expression of God's glory here is in the cross and the events that follow it (12:23-24). We see God's heart, and most fully understand what God was like, when we look at the cross where God gave his Son so we could have life.

2. Worship "in the Spirit" in John 4:23-24

Ancient Judaism often focused on the Spirit's work in inspiring prophecy. The Old Testament speaks of inspired, prophetic worship (e.g., 1 Sam. 10:5), especially in David's temple (1 Chron. 25:1-6). To "worship God in the Spirit," then, may involve trusting the Spirit of God to empower us for worship truly worthy of our awesome God. Given the general belief that the prophetic Spirit was no longer active to this extent in Jesus' day, Jesus' words would have struck his contemporaries forcefully.

3. God's message in the Tabernacle

Egyptians built temples differently than Mesopotamians; because the Israelites had been slaves in Egypt used in building projects, they undoubtedly knew what Egyptian temples looked like. They would have known about portable tent-shrines used in Egypt and Midian, as well as about the structure of Egyptian temples (and palaces), with an outer court, inner court, and the innermost shrine, the holiest place. God chose a design with which the Israelites were familiar so they could understand that the tabernacle they carried through the wilderness was a temple.

Some aspects of the tabernacle parallel other temples, and the parallels communicate true theology about God. In the tabernacle, the most expensive materials were used nearest the ark of the covenant: gold was more expensive than copper, and blue dye than red dye. These details reflect an ancient Near Eastern practice: people used the most expensive materials nearest the innermost sanctuary to signify that their god should be approached with awe and reverence. The tabernacle uses standard ancient Near Eastern symbols to communicate its point about God's holiness.

Some aspects of the tabernace include both parallels and contrasts, which also communicate theology about God. For instance, some of the furniture of the Tabernacle resembles the furniture of other ancient temples: a table of offerings, an altar, and so forth. But Canaanite, Egyptian and Hittite temples included other features like a chest of drawers and bed. Priests would wake their idols in the morning, give them their morning toilet, entertain them with dancing girls, feed them, and eventually put them back to bed at night. There was none of this in the Lord's temple, for he was not merely an idol dependent on his priests to assist him.

Some features of the tabernacle contrast starkly with their culture. The climax of other ancient Near Eastern and northern African temples was the image of the deity, enthroned on its sacred pedestal in the holiest innermost sanctuary; but there is no image in God's temple, because he would allow no graven images of himself (Ex 20:4). Further, many massive Egyptian temples included shrines for tutelary deities flanking the inner sanctuary; but there are no other deities associated with the Lord's tabernacle, for he would tolerate the worship of no other gods in his sight (Ex 20:3). God communicated his theology to Israel even in the architecture of the tabernacle, and he did so in cultural terms they could understand. (Some of the modern interpretations of the colors and design of the tabernacle are simply guesses that have become widely circulated. The suggestions we offer here represent instead careful research into the way temples were designed in Moses' day.)

4. Why Sarah used Hagar's womb and later expelled her

As an Egyptian, Hagar may have been one of the servants Pharaoh gave to Abraham and Sarah several years earlier (Gen 12:16). (Some of those Egyptians would have been from southern Egypt or Nubia.) In passing, we should note what the presence of Egyptian servants of Abraham implies for the matter of some African elements in Israel's ancestry. Abraham later passed his entire estate on to Isaac (25:5); when Jacob went down to Egypt with "seventy" people in his immediate family (46:27), this number does not include all the servants who also went with him, who were presumably retained as slaves when the Israelites were later enslaved (Ex 1:11). This means that the later Israelites included much Egyptian blood, in addition to the two half-tribes of Joseph (Gen 41:50).

But returning to the matter of Hagar: in some ancient Near Eastern cultures, if a woman could not bear her husband a son some other way, she might have her servant do it for her. So Sarah, following some assumptions of her culture, had Abraham get Hagar pregnant (16:2-3). In such cases, however, it was understood that the child would be legally the child of Sarah; but Hagar began to boast against Sarah as if she were better than Sarah (16:4).

After Isaac is born, Sarah finds Ishmael mocking him (21:9), and she realizes that Ishmael's presence threatens the birthright of the son God had promised, Isaac. According to some ancient Near Eastern customs, if Abraham had regarded Ishmael as his son, Ishmael would be treated as his firstborn. The way to prevent this was to free Hagar before Abraham's death, and send her and Ishmael away without the inheritance (21:10).

It was Sarah's initial suggestion that got Hagar in trouble, Hagar's arrogance that perpetuated it, but in the end, Sarah did act to preserve God's promise that she had endangered by her previous suggestion to Abraham. With the exception of Jesus, all biblical characters, including Abraham, Sarah and Hagar, were flawed in some ways; but understanding the customs of their day helps us better understand the decisions Sarah made.

5. Matthew 2:1-16

Ancient narrators often taught moral lessons by contrasting various characters, some good, some bad, and some mixed. In this narrative, there are three characters or sets of characters that warrant special attention in 2:1-6. They are the Magi ("wise men"), Herod the Great, and the scribes.

Magi were a caste of Persian astrologers--that is, they practiced a profession explicitly forbidden in the Old Testament (Deut 18:10; Is 47:13). The term is actually used in Greek translations of the Old Testament to describe Daniel's enemies who wanted to kill him! One of their jobs as Magi was to promote the honor of the king of Persia, whose official title was "king of kings and lord of lords." But these Magi come to honor the true king of kings born in Judea. Matthew thus shocks his Jewish-Christian readers by telling them of pagans who came to worship Jesus, implying that we cannot predict beforehand who will respond to our message; we must share it with everyone.

Herod the Great was a ruthless ruler who was paranoid about anyone threatening his kingship. Not being Jewish by birth (he was a descendant of the ancient Edomites) he was insecure about his title, "King of the Judeans," and did not want to share it with anyone else. He had two of his sons executed because he was told they were plotting against him (it turned out to be false), and another son executed for plotting against him--while Herod himself was dying. ("Better to be Herod's pig than his son," the emperor was reported to have complained.) A young high priest who was getting too popular and might have provided competition for Herod had a drowning accident--in a very shallow pool. Herod was the sort of person that this narrative describes! But killing the male children of Bethlehem (given Bethlehem's population in this period, maybe twenty boys) recalls how Pharaoh treated Israelite boys in Exodus. The pagan Magi worshiped the true king of the Jews; Herod the king of God's people, however, acted like a pagan king.

Most troubling of all, however, are the leading priests and scribes (2:4). These were the Bible professors and leading ministers of their day. They know where the Messiah will be born (2:5-6), but do not join the Magi on their quest. The people who knew the Bible the best took it for granted--a sin that only people who know the Bible can commit. And a generation later, when Jesus could no longer be taken for granted, their successors wanted him dead (Matt 26:3-4). The line between taking Jesus for granted and wanting him out of our way may remain rather thin today as well. Especially when background helps us learn more about the characters in this narrative, it warns us in stark terms not to prejudge who will respond to the gospel--and not to think of ourselves more highly than we ought.

6. Keeping God's Word in Matthew 5:18-19

In 5:18, Jesus says that not the smallest letter or mark will pass from God's law. He probably refers at least partly to the yod, the smallest letter in the

Hebrew alphabet. Later rabbis told the story that when God changed Sarai's name to Sarah, the yod that was removed complained to God for generations till he reinserted it, this time in Joshua's name. Some teachers also said that Solomon tried to uproot a *yod* from the Bible, whereon God announced that a thousand Solomons would be uprooted, but not a single *yod*. Jewish teachers used illustrations like this to make the point that the law was sacred and one could not regard any part as too small to be worthy of keeping.

When Jesus goes on to say that breaking the least command makes one least in the kingdom whereas keeping it makes one great in the kingdom, a prosaic modern reader might ask, "What happens if you break one and keep another?" But such a question misses the point of this typically Jewish language. Later rabbis decided that the greatest commandment was honoring one's father and mother, and the least, respecting a mother bird; they reasoned that both merited the same reward, eternal life (based on "life" in Ex. 20:12; Deut. 22:7). Thus if one broke the least commandment, one would be damned; if one kept it, one would be saved. Yet these same sages recognized that everyone sinned, including themselves. They were not saying that some people never broke any commandments; rather, they were saying that people could not pick and choose among the commandments. One could not say, "I am righteous because I do not kill, even though I have sex with someone I am not married to." Nor could one say, "I am godly because I do not steal, even though I cheat." All of God's commandments are his word, and to cast off any is to deny his right to rule over us, hence to reject him. Thus Jesus was saying in a similarly graphic way, "You cannot disregard even the smallest commandment, or God will hold you accountable."

7. The Kingdom Prayer in Matthew 6:9-13

Many pagans added up as many names of their deities as possible, reminding the deities of all their sacrifices and how the deities were therefore obligated in some sense to answer them. Jesus, however, says that we should predicate our prayers instead on the relationship our heavenly Father has given us with himself: we can cry out to him because he is our Father (Matt 6:7-9).

Jesus used some things in his culture, which was already full of biblical knowledge. Jesus here adapts a common synagogue prayer, that went something like this: "Our Father in heaven, exalted and hallowed be your great and glorious name, and may your kingdom come speedily and soon..." Jewish people expected a time when God's name would be "hallowed," or shown to be holy, among all peoples. For Jewish people, there was a sense in which God reigns in the present, but when they prayed for the coming of God's kingdom they were praying for him to rule unchallenged over all the earth and his will to be done on earth just as it is in heaven. Jesus therefore taught his disciples to pray for God's reign to come soon, when God's name would be universally honored.

To ask God for "daily bread" recalls how God provided bread each day for Israel in the wilderness; God is still our provider. To ask God to forgive our "debts" would stir a familiar image for many of Jesus' hearers. Poor peasants had to borrow much money to sow their crops, and Jesus' contemporaries understood that our sins were debts before God. To ask God not to "lead us into temptation" probably recalls a Jewish synagogue prayer of the day which asked God to preserve people from sinning. If so, the prayer might mean not, "Let us not be tested," but rather, "Do not let us fail the test" (compare 26:41, 45).

8. Enemy Soldiers Torture and Mock Jesus in Matthew 27:27-34

Over six hundred Roman soldiers were staying at the Fortress Antonia and at Pilate's palace (which once belonged to Herod the Great). Not recognizing that the true king of Israel and humanity stood before them, they mocked him as a pretend king. Roman soldiers were known for abusing and taunting prisoners; one ancient form of mockery was to dress someone as a king. Since soldiers wore red robes, they probably used a faded soldier's cloak to imitate the purple robe of earlier Greek rulers. People venerating such rulers would kneel before them, as here. Military floggings often used bamboo canes, so the soldiers may have had one available they could use as a mock king's sceptre. "Hail!" was the standard salute people gave to the Roman Emperor.

Spitting on a person was one of the most grievous insults a person could offer, and Jewish people considered the spittle of non-Jews particularly unclean. Romans stripped their captives naked-- especially shameful for Palestinian Jews; then they hanged the convict publicly.

Normally the condemned person was to carry the horizontal beam (Latin *patibulum*) of the cross himself, out to the site where the upright stake (Latin *palus*) awaited him; but Jesus' back had been too severely scourged beforehand for him to do this (27:26). Such scourgings often left the flesh of the person's back hanging down in bloody strips, sometimes left his bones showing, and sometimes led to the person's death from shock and blood loss. Thus the soldiers had to draft Simon of Cyrene to carry the crossbeam. Cyrene, a large city in what is now Libya in North Africa, had a large Jewish community (perhaps one quarter of the city) which no doubt included local converts. Like multitudes of foreign Jews and converts, Simon had come to Jerusalem for the feast. Roman soldiers could "impress" any person into service to carry things for them. Despite Jesus' teaching in Matthew 16:24, the soldiers had to draft a bystander to do what Jesus' disciples proved unwilling to do.

Crucifixion was the most shameful and painful form of execution known in the Roman world. Unable to privately excrete his wastes the dying person would excrete them publicly. Sometimes soldiers tied the condemned person to the cross; at other times they nailed them, as with Jesus. The dying man thus could not swat away insects attracted to his bloodied back or other wounds. Crucifixion victims sometimes took three days to finish dying.

The women of Jerusalem prepared a pain-killing potion of drugged wine for condemned men to drink; Jesus refused it (cf. 26:29). The myrrh-mixed wine of Mark 15:23, a delicacy and possibly an external pain reliever, becomes wine mixed with gall in Matthew; cf. Ps. 69:21 and the similarity between the Aramaic word for "myrrh" and Hebrew for "gall." Even without myrrh, wine itself was a painkiller (Prov 31:6-7). But Jesus refused it. Though we forsook him and fled when he needed us most, he came to bear our pain, and chose to bear it in full measure. Such is God's love for us all.

172

9. Adultery and Murder in Mark 6:17-29

Herod Antipas's affair with his sister-in-law Herodias, whom he had by this time married, was widely known. Indeed, the affair had led him to plan to divorce his first wife, whose father, a king, later went to war with Herod because of this insult and defeated him. John's denunciation of the affair as unlawful (Lev. 20:21) challenged Herod's sexual immorality, but Herod Antipas could have perceived it as a political threat, given the political ramifications that later led to a major military defeat. (The ancient Jewish historian Josephus claims that many viewed Herod's humiliation in the war as divine judgment for him executing John the Baptist.)

Celebrating birthdays was at this time a Greek and Roman but not a Jewish custom, but Jewish aristocrats had absorbed a large amount of Greek culture by this period. Other sources confirm that the Herodian court indulged in the sort of immoral behavior described here. After taking his brother's wife (Lev. 20:21), Antipas lusts after his wife's daughter Salome (cf. Lev. 20:14). He then utters the sort of oath one might give while drunk, but which especially recalls that of the Persian king stirred by Queen Esther's beauty (Esther 5:3, 6, 7:2), though this girl's request will be far less noble. But as a Roman vassal Herod had no authority to give any of his kingdom away anyway.

Salome had to go "out" to ask her mother Herodias because women and men normally dined separately at banquets. Excavations at Antipas's fortress Machaerus suggest two dining halls, one for women and one for men; Herodias thus was probably not present to watch Herod's reaction to the dance. Josephus characterizes Herodias the same way Mark does: a jealous, ambitious schemer.

Although Romans and their agents usually executed lower class persons and slaves by crucifixion or other means, the preferred form of execution for respectable people was beheading. By asking for John's head on a platter, however, Salome wanted it served up as part of the dinner menu--a ghastly touch of ridicule. Although Antipas's oath was not legally binding and Jewish sages could release him from it, it would have proved embarrassing to break an oath before dinner guests; even the emperor would not lightly do that. Most people were revolted by leaders who had heads brought to them, but many accounts confirm that powerful tyrants like Antipas had such things done.

If a man had sons, normally the eldest son was responsible for his father's burial; here, John's disciples must fulfill this role for him. Since he had been executed, the disciples performed a dangerous task unless they had Herod's permission to take the body. Their courage underlines by way of contrast the abandonment of Jesus' male disciples during his burial!

10. A New King's Birthday in Luke 2:1-14

Censuses were used especially to evaluate taxation requirements. A tax census instigated by the revered emperor Augustus here begins the narrative's contrast between Caesar's earthly pomp and Christ's heavenly glory. Although Egyptian census records show that people had to return to their homes for a tax census, the "home" to which they returned was where they owned property, not simply where they were born (censuses registered persons according to property). Joseph thus must have still held property in Bethlehem. Betrothal provided most of the legal rights of marriage, but intercourse was forbidden; Joseph was courageous to take his pregnant betrothed with him, even if (as is quite possible) she was also a Bethlehemite who had to return to that town. Although tax laws in most of the Empire only required the head of a household to appear, the province of Syria (then including Judea) also taxed women. But Joseph may have simply wished to avoid leaving her alone this late in her pregnancy, especially if the circumstances of her pregnancy had deprived her of other friends.

The "swaddling clothes" were long cloth strips used to keep babies' limbs straight so they could grow properly. Midwives normally assisted at birth;

especially since this was Mary's first child, it is likely
(though not clear from the text) that a midwife would
have been found to assist her. Jewish law permitted
midwives to travel a long distance even on the Sabbath
to assist in delivery.

By the early second century even pagans were
widely aware of the tradition that Jesus was born in
a cave used as a livestock shelter behind someone's
home. The manger was a feeding trough for animals;
sometimes these may have been built into the floor.
The traditional "inn" could as easily be translated
"home" or "guest room," and probably means that,
since many of Joseph's scattered family members had
returned to the home at once, it was easier for Mary to
bear in the vacant cave outside.

Many religious people and especially the social
elite in this period generally despised shepherds as a
low-class occupation; but God sees differently than
people do. Pasturing of flocks at night indicates that
this was a warmer season, not winter (when they
would graze more in the day); December 25 was later
adopted as Christmas only to supercede a pagan
Roman festival scheduled at that time.

Pagans spoke of the "good news" of the emperor's
birthday, celebrated throughout the empire; they
hailed the emperor as "Savior" and "Lord." They used
choirs in imperial temples to worship the emperor.

They praised the current emperor, Augustus, for having inaugurated a worldwide "peace." But the lowly manger distinguishes the true king from the Roman emperor; Jesus is the true Savior, Lord, bringer of universal peace. God is not impressed with human power or honor; he came as the lowliest of all among the lowliest of all, revealing God's special heart toward those who most depend on him for their help.

11. Demands of Discipleship in Luke 9:58-62

Warning a prospective disciple that the Son of Man has less of a home than foxes and birds indicates that those who follow him may lack the same securities. Disciples usually sought out their own teachers (in contrast to Jesus, who called some of his own). Some radical philosophers who eschewed possessions sought to repulse prospective disciples with enormous demands, for the purpose of testing them and acquiring only the most worthy disciples. Many Palestinian Jews were poor, but few were homeless; Jesus had given up even home to travel and was completely dependent on the hospitality and support of others.

The man who wants to bury his father is not asking for a short delay: his father has not died that day or the day before. Family members carried the body to the tomb shortly after its death and then remained at home for seven days to mourn. The man could be saying, as in some similar Middle Eastern cultures,

"Let me wait until my father dies someday and I fulfill my obligation to bury him." The other possibility is that he refers to his father's *second* burial, a custom practiced precisely in this period. A year after the first burial, after the flesh had rotted off the bones, the son would return to *rebury* the bones in a special box in a slot in the wall. This son could thus be asking for as much as a year's delay.

One of an eldest son's most basic responsibities was his father's burial. Jesus' demand that the son place Jesus above the greatest responsibility a son could offer his father would thus have defied the social order: in Jewish tradition, honoring father and mother was one of the greatest commandments, and to follow Jesus in such a radical way would have seemed like breaking this commandment.

But while the second inquirer learned the priority of following Jesus, the third learns the *urgency* of following Jesus. One prospective disciple requests merely permission to say farewell to his family, but Jesus compares this request with looking back from plowing, which would cause one to ruin one's furrow in the field. Jesus speaks figuratively to remind his hearer of the story of Elisha's call. When Elijah found Elisha plowing, he called him to follow him, but allowed him to first bid farewell to his family (1 Kings 19:19-21). The Old Testament prophets sacrificed much to serve God's will, but Jesus' call here is more radical than that of a radical prophet! Although we must beware of others who sometimes misrepresent Jesus' message, we must be willing to pay any price that Jesus' call demands on our lives.

12. God's Friends Rejoice in Luke 15:18-32

The religious elite were angry with Jesus for spending time with tax-gatherers and sinners; after all, Scripture warned against spending time with ungodly people (Ps 1:1; Prov 13:20). The difference, of course, is that Jesus is spending time with sinners to influence them for the kingdom, not to be shaped by their ways (Lk 15:1-2).

Jesus answered the religious elite by telling them three stories: the story of the lost sheep, the lost coin, and the lost son. A hundred was roughly an average sized flock, and when one sheep strayed the shepherd would do whatever necessary to recover it. (He could leave his other sheep with fellow shepherds who would watch over their flocks together with him. Sheep would often roam together and be separated by their shepherds' distinctive calls or flutes.) When he finds what was lost, he calls his friends together to rejoice, and Jesus says it is the same way with God: those who are really his friends rejoice with him when he regains what was lost (15:3-7). The implication seems to be that the religious elite are not God's friends, or they would be rejoicing.

Jesus then turns to the story of the lost coin. If a woman had ten coins as her dowry, the money she had brought into her marriage in case of divorce or widowhood, she was a very poor woman indeed: ten coins represented about ten days' wages for the average working man. In any case, one out of ten is more than one out of a hundred, and she is desperate to find the coin! Most small, one-room Galilean homes had floors of roughly fitted stones, so coins and other objects routinely fell between the cracks and remained lost until excavated by modern archaeologists! Further, most of these homes had at most one small window and a doorway, so there was little light to help her find her coin. She thus lights a lamp, but in this period most lamps were small enough to hold in the palm of one's hand, and these did not provide much light. So she sweeps with a broom, hoping to hear it tinkle--and finally, she finds it! Her friends rejoice with her, just as God's friends rejoice with him--implying, again, that perhaps the religious elite are not among God's friends (15:8-10).

Jesus then turns to the story of the lost son. The younger son says to his father, "I want my share of the inheritance now." In that culture, the son was virtually declaring, "Father, I wish you were dead"--the epitome of disrespect. The father was under no obigation to divide his inheritance, but he divided it anyway; the elder brother would have received two thirds and the younger one third. Under ancient law, by dividing the inheritance the father simply was telling them which fields and items each would get after his decease; the son could not legally *spend* the estate before then. But this son does it anyway; he flees to a far country and wastes his father's years of work. In the end, however, reduced to poverty, he has to feed pigs; for Jesus' Jewish hearers, this was a fitting end for such a rebellious son, and a fitting end for the story. If the young man were involved with pigs, he would be unclean and not even be able to approach fellow Jews for help!

But the young man decides that he would rather be a servant in his father's house than starve, so he returns home to beg for mercy. His father, seeing him a long way off, runs to meet him. In that culture, it was considered undignified for older men to run, but this father discards his dignity; his son has come home! The son tries to plead that he might be a slave, but the father ignores him, instead calling for the best robe in the house--undoubtedly his own; and a ring for the young man's finger--undoubtedly a signet ring, symbolizing his reinstatement to sonship; and sandals for his feet--because most servants did not wear sandals, the father is saying, "No, I will not receive you as a servant! I will receive you *only* as my son!" The fatted calf was enough food to feed the entire village, so he throws a big party, and all his friends rejoice with him.

So far the story has paralleled the two stories that preceded it, but now Jesus goes further, challenging the religious elite more directly. Ancient literature sometimes framed an important paragraph by starting and ending on the same statement, here that his lost son has come home (15:24, 32). When the elder brother discovers that the father has welcomed home his younger brother, he has nothing to lose economically; the inheritance was already divided (15:12). The problem is that he regards as unfair his father celebrating the return of a rebellious son when he himself needed no mercy; he thought himself good enough *without* his father's mercy. He protests to his father, refusing to greet him with a title, reducing the father to coming out and begging him to come in. He is now disrespecting his father just as much as the younger brother had earlier! "I have been serving you," he protests (15:29), thereby revealing that he saw himself as a servant rather than a son--the very role the father refused to consider acceptable (15:21-22).

The religious elite despised the "sinners" who were coming to Jesus, not realizing that their hearts were no better. The sinners were like the younger brother, the religious elite like the older one. All of us need Jesus; none can be saved without God's mercy.

13. The First Gentile Christian in Acts 8:26-27

Since Samaritans were considered half-breeds (8:4-25), this African court official is the first fully Gentile convert to Christianity (though probably unknown to most of the Jerusalem church, 11:18).

The angel's instructions to go south toward Gaza (8:26) probably would have seemed strange to Philip; Samaria yielded many converts, but who would he find on a generally deserted road? Two roads led south from near Jerusalem, one through Hebron into Idumea (Edom) and the other joining the coast road before Gaza heading for Egypt, both with many Roman milestones as road-markers. Old Gaza was a deserted town whose ruins lay near the now culturally Greek cities of Askelon and New Gaza. The command to head south for a few days toward a deserted city may have seemed absurd; but God had often tested faith through seemingly absurd commands (e.g., Exod. 14:16; 1 Kings 17:3-4, 9-14; 2 Kings 5:10).

"Ethiopia" (a Greek term) figured in Mediterranean legends and mythical geography as the very end of the earth, sometimes extending from the far south (all Africa south of Egypt, the "wooly-haired Ethiopians") to the far east (the "straight-haired Ethiopians" of southern India). Greek literature often respected Africans as a people particularly beloved by the gods (the Greek historian Herodotus also calls them the most handsome of people), and some sub-Sahara Africans were known in the Roman Empire. The most commonly mentioned feature of Ethiopians in Jewish and Greco-Roman literature (also noted in the Old Testament) is their black skin, though ancient Mediterranean art also depicted other typically African features and recognized differences in skin tone. Egyptians and other peoples were sometimes called "black" by comparison with lighter Mediterranean peoples, but the further south one traveled along the Nile, the darker the complexion and more tightly coiled the hair of the people. Greeks considered the "Ethiopians" the epitome of blackness.

Here a particular African empire is in view. While we might confuse "Ethiopia" here with modern Ethiopia, that is probably not in view. That kingdom, Axum, was a powerful east African empire and converted to Christianity in the early 300s, in the same generation the Roman empire converted. The empire here, however, is most likely a particular Nubian kingdom of somewhat darker complexion, south of Egypt in what is now the Sudan. "Candace" (*kan-dak'a*) seems to have been a dynastic title of the Queen of this Nubian Empire; she is mentioned elsewhere in Greco-Roman literature, and tradition declares that the queen-mother ruled in that land. (Ancient Greeks called all of Nubia "Ethiopia.") Her black Nubian kingdom had lasted since c. 750 BC; its main cities were Meroe and Napata. This kingdom was wealthy (giving a royal treasurer like this one much to do!) and had trade ties to the north; Rome procured peacocks and other African treasures through such African kingdoms in contact with the interior of Africa, and Roman wealth has turned up in excavations of Meroe. The trade also extended further south; a bust of Caesar has been found as far south as Tanzania. Still, the trade connection with Rome was limited, and this official and his entourage must have been among the few Nubian visitors this far north.

This Nubian court official was probably a Gentile "God-fearer." When meant literally--which was not always the case (Gen. 39:1 LXX), eunuchs referred to castrated men. Although these were preferred court officials in the East, the Jewish people opposed the practice, and Jewish law excluded eunuchs from Israel (Deut. 23:1); the rules were undoubtedly instituted to prevent Israel from neutering boys (Deut. 23:1). But eunuchs could certainly be accepted by God (Isa. 56:3-5, even foreign eunuchs; Wisd. 3:14). An Ethiopian "eunuch" in the OT turns out to be one of Jeremiah's few allies and saves his life (Jer. 38:7-13). This African court official was the first non-Jewish Christian. Such information may be helpful in establishing that Christianity is not only not a western religion, but that after its Jewish origins it was first of all an African faith.

14. Paul preaches to Philosophers in Acts 17:22-31

Paul "contextualized" the gospel for his hearers, showing how it related to their own culture without compromising its content. (Today we often err on either one side or the other--failing to be culturally relevant, or failing to represent accurately the biblical message.) Paul speaks to two groups of philosophers present, Stoics and (probably a smaller group) Epicureans; his faith held little common ground with Epicureans, but the Stoics could agree with a number of Cn beliefs.

Paul opens by finding some common ground with his pagan audience. It was customary to begin a speech by complimenting the hearers in the opening of a speech, the *exordium*. One was not permitted to flatter the Areopagus (the leading philosophical and educational leaders of Athens), but Paul would remain free to start on a respectful note. "Religious" meant that they were observant, not that he agreed with their religion ("superstitious," in the King James Version, does not convey the right idea).

Then Paul turns to more common ground. During a plague long before Paul's lifetime, no altars had successfully propitiated the gods; finally Athens had offered sacrifices to an unknown god, immediately staying the plague. These altars were still standing, and Paul uses this as the basis for his speech.

Paul borrows a technique from Jewish teachers who had been trying to explain the true God to Gentiles for several centuries before Paul. Non-Palestinian Jews sometimes reminded Gentiles that even they had one supreme God, and tried to show pagans that their highest religious aspirations were best met in Judaism. Stoics believed that God permeated all things and therefore was not localized in temples (cf. also Is 66:1). Stoics and Greek-speaking Judaism emphasized that God "needs nothing," using the same word Paul uses in 17:25. Jews and many Greeks alike agreed that God was creator and divider of the earth's boundaries and of seasons' boundaries (17:26). (Stoics also believed that the universe periodically dissolved back into God, but on this there was no point of contact between them and the Bible or Judaism.)

Jewish people usually spoke of God as a father specifically to his people. But Greeks, Jews scattered among Greeks, and some second-century Christian writers spoke of God as the world's "father" in the sense of creator; though Paul elsewhere uses the term more specifically, he adopts the more general sense of father as creator in this case (17:28-29). The quote from Epimenides in 17:28 appears in Jewish anthologies of proof-texts useful for showing pagans the truth about God, and Paul may have learned it there. (Greeks cited Homer and other poets as proof-texts in a manner similar to how Jewish people cited Scripture.)

But while Paul was eager to find points of contact with the best in pagan thinking for the sake of communicating the gospel, he also was clear where the gospel disagreed with paganism. Some issues might be semantic, but Paul would not ignore any real differences. Although philosophers spoke of conversion to philosophy through a change of thinking, they were unfamiliar with his Jewish and Christian doctrine of repentance towards God (17:30). Further, the Greek view of time was that it would simply continue, not that there was a future climax of history in the day of judgment, in contrast to the biblical perspective (17:31). Finally, Greeks could not conceive of a future bodily resurrection; most of them simply believed the soul survived after death. Thus Paul's preaching of the resurrection offended them most (17:31-32). But in the end, Paul was more interested in winning at least a few of these influential people to genuine faith in Christ (17:34) than in simply persuading all of them that he was harmless and shared their own views.

15. Paul Adapts Ancient Family Rules in Ephesians 5:21-6:9

Some people used Ephesians 6:5-9 alongside Greek, Roman, and Arab discussions of slavery to support the kind of slavery practiced in the Americas, but a simple knowledge of the nature of the slavery Paul addressed would have disproved their understanding of the passage. Others even more recently have used

5:22-33 to treat wives in disrespectful and demeaning ways, which also misinterprets the entire tenor of the passage.

This passage addresses an ancient sort of writing called "household codes," by which Paul's readers could try to convince their prospective persecutors that they were not subversives after all. In Paul's day, many Romans were troubled by the spread of "religions from the East" (such as Egyptian Isis worship, Judaism, and Christianity) which they thought would undermine traditional Roman family values. Members of these minority religions often tried to show their support for those values by using a standard form of exhortations developed by philosophers from Aristotle on.

From the time of Aristotle onward these exhortations instructed the male head of a household how to deal with members of his family, especially how he should rule his wife, children, and slaves. Paul borrows this form of discussion straight out of standard Greco-Roman moral writing, even following their sequence. But unlike most ancient writers, Paul changes the basic premise of these codes: the absolute authority of the male head of the house.

That Paul introduces the household codes with a command to mutual submission (5:21) is significant. In his day it was customary to call on wives, children and slaves to submit in various ways, but calling *all* members of a group (including the *pater familias*, the male head of the household) to submit to one another was unheard of.

Most ancient writers expected wives to obey their husbands, desiring in them a quiet and meek demeanor; sometimes a requirement for absolute obedience was even stated in the marriage contracts. This made sense especially to Greek thinkers, who could not conceive of wives as equals. Age differences contributed to this disparity: husbands were normally substantially older than their wives, often by over a decade in Greek culture (with men frequently marrying around 30 and women in their teens, often early teens).

In this passage, however, Paul adapts the traditional code in several ways. First, wifely submission is rooted in Christian submission in general (in Greek, 5:22 even borrows its verb "submit" from 5:21); submission is a Christian virtue, but not only for wives! Second, Paul addresses not only husbands but also wives, which most household codes did not. Third, whereas household codes told the husbands how to make their wives obey them, Paul simply tells husbands how to *love* their wives. Finally, the closest Paul comes to *defining* submission in this context is "respect" (5:33). At the same time that he relates Christianity to the standards of his culture, he actually transforms his culture's values by going so far beyond them! Paul addressed Greco-Roman culture, but few cultures today give precisely the same expressions of submission as in his culture. Today Christians reapply his principles in different ways for different cultures, but these principles still contradict many practices in many of our cultures (such as beating a wife).

No one would have disagreed with Paul's premise in 6:1-4: Jewish and Greco-Roman writers unanimously agreed that children needed to honor their parents, and, at least till they grew up, needed to obey them as well. At the same time, Greek and Roman fathers and teachers often instructed children with beatings. Paul is among the minority of ancient writers who seem to warn against being too harsh in discipline (6:4). (Greek and Roman society was even harsher on newborn children; since an infant was accepted as a legal person only when the father officially recognized it, babies could be abandoned or, if deformed, killed. Early Christians and Jews unanimously opposed both abortion and abandonment. This text, however, addresses the discipline of minors in the household, as in the household codes.) Disobedience might be permitted under some exceptional circumstances (e.g., 1 Sam 20:32), but Paul does not qualify the traditional Roman view on children's submission as he does with wives and slaves, since the Old Testament also mandated minors' submission (Deut 21:18-21).

Finally, Paul addresses relations between slaves and slaveholders. Roman slavery, unlike later European slavery and much of (though not all of) Arab slavery, was nonracial; the Romans were happy to enslave anyone who was available. Different forms of slavery existed in Paul's day. Banishment to slavery in the mines or gladiatorial combat was virtually a death sentence; few slaves survived long under such circumstances. Slaves who worked the fields could be beaten, but otherwise were very much like free peasants, who also were harshly oppressed and barely ever were able to advance their position socially, though they comprised the bulk of the Empire's population. Household slaves, however, lived under conditions better than those of free peasants. They could earn money on the side and often purchased their freedom; once free they could be promoted socially, and their former slaveholder owed them obligations to help them succeed socially. Many freedpersons became wealthier than aristocrats. Ranking slaves in some wealthy households could wield more power than free aristocrats. Some nobles, for example, married into slavery to become slaves in Caesar's household and improve their social and economic position! Household codes addressed household slaves, and Paul writes to urban congregations, so the sort of slavery he addresses here is plainly household slavery.

Slaveholders often complained that slaves were lazy, especially when no one was looking. Paul encourages hard work, but gives the slave a new hope and a new motive for his or her labor (6:5-8). (In general, Paul believes we should submit to those in authority, when that is possible, for the sake of peace--cf. Rom 12:18; 13:1-7; but that does not mean that he believes we should work to maintain such authority structures; cf. I Cor 7:20-23.) Paul says that slaves, like wives, should submit to the head of the household as if to Christ (6:5), but again makes clear that this is a *reciprocal* duty; slaves and slaveholders both share the same heavenly master. When Aristotle complained about a few philosophers who think that slavery is wrong, the philosophers he cited did not state matters as plainly as Paul does here. Only a very small minority of writers in the ancient world (many of them Stoics) suggested that slaves were in theory their masters' spiritual equals, but Paul goes beyond even this extreme: only Paul goes so far as to suggest that in practice masters do the same for slaves as slaves should do for them (6:9a). (Jewish Essenes opposed slavery, but that was because they opposed private property altogether!)

Some have complained that Paul should have opposed slavery more forcefully. But in the few verses in which Paul addresses slaves, he confronts only the practical issue of how slaves can deal with their situation, not with the legal institution of slavery--the same way a minister or counselor today might help someone get free from an addiction without ever having reason to discuss the legal issues related to that addiction. The only attempts to free all slaves in the Roman Empire before him had been three massive slave wars, all of which had ended in widespread bloodshed without liberating the slaves. Christians at this point were a small persecuted minority sect whose only way to abolish slavery would be to persuade more people of their cause and transform the values of the Empire (the way the abolitionist movement spread in eighteenth and nineteenth century Britain). Further, even if this specific letter were intended as a critique of social injustice (which is not the purpose of this particular letter, though that topic arises in other biblical passages), one would not start such a critique with household slaves, but with mine slaves, and then both free peasants and agrarian slaves. ven a violent revolution could not have ended slavery in the Roman Empire. In any event, what Paul does say leaves no doubt where he would have stood had we put the theoretical question of slavery's abolition to him: people are equals before God (6:9), and slavery is therefore against God's will.

16. Jesus Rebukes the Self-Sufficient in Revelation 3:15-18

Laodicea became an important Phrygian city in Roman times. It was capital of the Cibryatic convention, including at least 25 towns. It was also the wealthiest city in Phrygia, and especially prosperous in this period. It was 10 miles west of Colosse and its rival city was Phrygian Antioch. The city reflected the usual paganism of the larger Mediterranean culture: Zeus was the city's patron deity, but Laodiceans also had temples for Apollo, Asclepius (the healing deity), Hades, Hera, Athena, Serapis, Dionysus, and other deities. The church seemed to share the values of its culture, an arrogant self-sufficiency in matters including its prosperity, clothing and health, all of which Jesus challenges in 3:17-18. Laodicea was a prosperous banking center; proud of its wealth, it refused Roman disaster relief after the earthquake of AD 60, rebuilding from its own resources. It was also known for its textiles (especially black wool) and for its medical school with ear medicine and undoubtedly the highly reputed Phrygian eye salve. Everything in which Laodicea could have confidence outwardly, her church, which reflected its culture, lacked spiritually.

The one sphere of life in which Laodiceans could not pretend to be self-sufficient was their water supply! Laodicea had to pipe in its water from elsewhere, and by the time it arrived it was full of sediment; Laodicea actually acquired a bad reputation for its water supply. Jesus comments on the temperature of the water: they were lukewarm, neither cold nor hot. This does not mean, as some have suggested, that hot water was good but cold water was bad; Jesus would not want the Laodiceans "good or bad," but only good. Cold water was preferred for drinking, and hot water for bathing (also sometimes drunk at banquets), but the natural lukewarmness of local water (in contrast with the hot water available at nearby Hierapolis or cold water of nearby mountains) was undoubtedly a standard complaint of local residents, most of whom had an otherwise comfortable lifestyle. Jesus is saying: "Were you hot or cold, you would be useful; but as it is, you are simply disgusting. I feel toward you the way you feel toward your water supply--you make me sick."

The above examples of cultural background are merely samples, but hopefully they have given you an appetite for more. Background sheds light on each passage in the Bible. This is a goal, of course, not a matter on which each interpreter will always agree. Paul recognized that we "know in part and prophesy in part" (1 Cor 13:9)--some texts remain obscure to us (but we have plenty of others to keep us busy till we can understand the obscurer ones). Until Jesus returns, we will never know eveything, and we need to be charitable in our disagreement with others whose conclusions differ from our own. That brings us back to some of our earlier comments: focus on what is most central and hardest to dispute, and deal with details only as you are able afterward.

Chapter 6
Context of Genre

Although we have surveyed and illustrated many of the most important *general* rules for interpretation, we must now note that some interpretation skills depend on the kinds of writing in the Bible one is studying. For example, Revelation is prophetic (and probably apocalyptic) literature, which is full of symbols; if interpreters today debate how literal some of Revelation's images are, no one doubts that much of Revelation (for instance, the prostitute and the bride) are each symbols representing something other than what they would mean literally (Babylon and New Jerusalem versus two literal women). The Psalms are poetry, and also often employ graphic images. Poetry involved poetic license; when Job claims that his steps were "bathed in butter" (Job 29:6), he means that he was prosperous, not that his hallways were packed with butter up to his ankles. One could provide hundreds of examples; those who deny the use of symbolism in some parts of the Bible (especially poetic portions) have simply not read the Bible very thoroughly.

On the other hand, narratives are not full of symbols. One should not read the story of David and Goliath and think, "What does Goliath stand for? What do the smooth stones stand for?" These accounts are intended as literal historical stories, and we seek to learn morals from these accounts the same way we would seek to learn them from our experiences or accounts of others' experiences today. (The difference between biblical experiences and modern experiences is that the biblical ones more often come with clues to the proper interpretation from God's perfect perspective.) We may apply what we learn from Goliath to other challenges that we face, but Goliath does not "symbolize" those challenges; he is simply one example of a challenge.

Even our most important rule, context, functions differently for different kinds of writings. Most proverbs, for instance, are not recorded in any noteworthy sequence providing a flow of thought; they are isolated, general sayings, and were simply collected (Prov 25:1). This is not to suppose, however, that we lack a larger context in which to read specific proverbs. By reading these proverbs in light of the entire collection of proverbs, and especially in light of other proverbs addressing the same topic, we have a general context available for most individual proverbs.

Scholars use the term "genre" for kinds of writings. Poetry, prophecy, history and wisdom saying are some of the genres represented in the Bible; examples of different kinds of genres exist today, for example fiction (most parables are something like fiction), bomb threats, or newspaper reports. Let us survey some of the most common "genres" in the Bible, and some important interpretation principles for each.

1. Narrative

Narrative is the most common genre in the Bible. Narrative simply means a "story," whether a true story like history or biography (most of the Bible's narratives) or a story meant to communicate truth by fictional analogy, like a parable. A basic rule of interpretation for a story is that we should ask, "What is the moral of this story?" Or to put it differently, "What lessons can we learn from this story?"

Avoid Allegory

Some principles help us draw lessons from stories accurately. The first principle is a warning, especially for historical narratives in the Bible: Do *not* allegorize the story. That is, do not turn it into a series of symbols as if it did not happen. If we turn a narrative into symbols, anyone can interpret the narrative to say whatever they want; people can read the same narrative and come up with opposite religions! When we read into a text in this way, we read into it what we already think--which means that we act like we do not need the text to teach us anything new!

For example, when David prepares to fight Goliath, he gathers five smooth stones. One allegorist might claim that David's five stones represent love, joy, peace, longsuffering, gentleness, and goodness. Another might claim that he picked five stones to represent five particular spiritual gifts; or perhaps five pieces of spiritual armor listed by Paul in the New Testament. But such interpretations are utterly unhelpful. First, they are unhelpful because anyone can come up with any interpretation, and there is no objective way for everyone to find the same point in the text. Second, they are unhelpful because it is really the allegorist and his views, rather than the text itself, which supplies its meaning and teaches something. Third, it is unhelpful because it obscures the real point of the text. Why did David pick smooth stones? They were easier to aim. Why did David pick five of them instead of one? Presumably in case he missed the first time; the lesson we learn from this example is that faith is not presumption: David knew God would use him to kill Goliath, but he did not know if he would kill him with the first stone.

Where did allegory come from? Some Greek philosophers grew embarrassed about the myths of their gods committing adultery, robbery, and murder, so they turned the myths into a series of symbols rather than taking them as true teachings about their gods. Some Jewish philosophers, trying to defend the Bible against accusations by Greeks, explained away uncomfortable portions of the Bible by taking them as mere symbols. Thus instead of allowing that biblical heroes like Noah had weaknesses, a Jewish philosopher might claim that he did not actually get drunk with wine, but rather was spiritually drunk on the wonderful knowledge of God. Christian scholars from Alexandria, whose schools were controlled by Greek philosophical thought, often practiced allegory, though some other church leaders (like John Chrysostom) preferred the literal meaning. Gnostics like Valentinus, condemned by the orthodox Christians, mixed some Christian ideas with pagan philosophy. They often used the allegorical method to justify blurring distinction between Christianity and other thought systems. Many later Christian thinkers borrowed the allegorical method, which became quite common especially in Europe in the Middle Ages.[1]

Many people practice allegory because they want to discover some hidden meaning in every word or phrase of Scripture, The problem with this approach is that it defies the way Scripture was actually given to us, hence disrespects rather than respects Scripture.

[1] On Gnostic use of allegory, see e.g., Stephen M. Miller, "Malcontents fro Christ," *Christian History* 51 (1996): 32-34, p. 32; Carl A. Volz, "The Genius of Chrysostom's Preaching," *Christian History* 44 (1994): 24-26, p. 24. For the Alexandrian school (perhaps a little too favorably), see Robert M. Grant with David Tracy, *A Short History of the Interpretation of the Bible*, 2d ed. (Philadelphia: Fortress, 1984), 52-62; on the Antiochenes like Chrysostom, see ibid., pp. 63-72.

The level of meaning is often the story as a whole, and individual words and phrases normally simply contribute to that larger contextual meaning. To read into the story meaning that is not there is in essence to attempt to *add* inspiration to Scripture, as if it were inadequate by itself. (Allegorical attempts to find a deeper meaning behind the actual words of Scripture takes on many forms. In recent years some have looked for numerical patterns in the words of Scripture, but these ignore the hundreds of "textual variants," mostly spelling differences, among different ancient copies of the Bible. Most scholars agree that the supposed number patterns some computer technicians have found in Scripture are random; one can come up with equally convincing results for other kinds of patterns.)

Read the Story as a Whole

Sometimes we cannot draw a correct moral from a story because we have picked too narrow a text. Earlier in this book I mentioned my friend who doubted the usefulness of the passage where Abishag lies in bed with David to keep him warm. What moral would we draw from such a story? We would be wrong if we supposed that the moral was that young people should lie with older people to keep them warm. True as it might be that we should look out for the health of our kings or other leaders, that is also not the moral. Nor is the moral that live humans work better than blankets? Some might wish to draw from it a lesson that contradicts other moral teachings in the Bible. But all these interpretations miss the point, because the writer did not intend us to read one paragraph of the story and then stop. We should read the entire story, and in the flow of the entire story, this paragraph identifies that David is dying and prepares us for why Solomon must later execute his treacherous brother Adonijah. It helps us understand the rest of the story, and the point comes from the larger story, not always all of its individual parts.

How much do we need to read to get the whole picture? As a general rule, the more context you read, the better. We need not spend much time here, because this is the principle of whole book context we illustrated at length above. We should pause merely to point out that the literary unit is sometimes longer than what appears as a book in our Bibles. Because it was difficult to get a very long document on a single scroll, longer works were often divided into smaller "books." Thus 1 Samuel through 2 Kings represents one continuous story (with smaller parts); 1 and 2 Chronicles represents anothert story; Luke and Acts together comprise a single, united work (although our Bibles place John between them; read Acts 1:1 with Lk 1:3).

There is also a sense in which larger stories may contain smaller ones. For example, many of the stories in Mark can be read on their own as self-contained units with their own morals; some scholars have argued that the early church used those stories as units for preaching the way they used many Old Testament readings. But while this observation is true, modern scholars recognize that we should also recognize these smaller stories in their larger context to get the most out of them; one can follow the development of and suspense in Mark's "plot" and trace the themes of the Gospel from start to finish. This prevents us from drawing the wrong applications. For instance, one might read Mark 1:45 and assume that if one is sent from God and fulfills God's mission like Jesus does, one will be popular with the masses. But if one reads the whole Gospel, one recognizes that the crowds later clamor for Jesus' execution (Mk 15:11-15). The moral is not that obedience to God always leads to popularity; the moral is that we cannot trust popularity to last, for the crowds are often easily swayed. Jesus thus focused on making disciples more than on drawing crowds (Mk 4:9-20).

Identify the Lessons in the Story

Reading a biblical story as a true account and then learning principles by analogy (the way we would learn lessons from hearing, say, our parents' stories of lessons they learned in life) is *not* allegorizing; it is reading these stories the way they were meant to be read. As best as possible, we should put ourselves in the place of the original audience of the story, read it in the context of the whole book it which it appears, and try to learn from it what the first audience would have. Only then are we ready to think how to reapply the story to our situations and needs today. At the same time, if we stop we the ancient meaning, we will miss the story's original impact. Once we understood what it meant in its first setting, we must think how to apply the passage with a comparable impact for our settings today.

Most narratives involve characters. One can try to determine whether the examples of the characters were good or bad ones in any given case by several methods: (1) When the writer and readers shared the same culture and it assumed an act was bad or good, the writer could assume that the readers knew which was which, unless he disagreed with the views of the culture. (2) If you read through the entire book, you may notice patterns of behavior; an evaluation of the behavior in one case would apply to similar cases of the behavior in that book. (3) By deliberately highlighting the differences among characters, one could usually see which were good and which were bad examples.

Sometimes we learn from a story by looking at positive and negative characters in the story and contrasting them. We can do this frequently in 1 Samuel; in chapters 1 and 2, we learn that humble Hannah, who was looked down on by many of the few people who knew her, was godly, whereas Eli the high priest had compromised his calling. Hannah offered to give up her son for God; Eli, refusing to give up his sons for God, ultimately lost them and everything else as well. After this the story compares the boy Samuel, who hears God and delivers his message, with Eli's ungodly sons, who abuse their ministry to make themselves rich and have sexual relations with many women. God ultimately exalts Samuel but kills the hypocritical ministers. Later 1 Samuel contrasts David and Saul; by examining the differences between them, we can learn principles for fulfilling God's call and also dangers to avoid.

Such contrasts also appear in the New Testament, for instance in Luke chapter 1. Zechariah was a respected, aged priest serving in the Jerusalem temple, but when Gabriel came to him Zechariah disbelieved and was struck mute for a few months. By contrast, the angel Gabriel next comes to Mary with an even more dramatic message, but she believes. On account of her gender, her age, her social status, and being in Nazareth rather than the temple, most people would think less highly of Mary than of Zechariah. But the narrative shows us that Mary responded with greater faith and consequently received greater blessing than Zechariah. Similarly, we noted above a contrast between the Magi who seek Jesus and Herod who seeks to kill him.

Of course, distinguishing positive from negative examples is not always simple, and most characters in the Bible, just like most characters in Greek histories and biography, included a mixture of positive and negative traits. The Bible tells us about real people, and we learn from that pattern as well not to idolize as perfect or demonize as wholly evil people today. John the Baptist was the greatest prophet before Jesus (Matt 11:11-14), but he was unsure whether Jesus was fulfilling his prophecy (Matt 11:2-3) because Jesus was healing sick people but not pouring out fiery judgment (Matt 3:11-12). John was a man of God, but he did not know that the kingdom would come in two stages because its king would come twice. Distinguishing positive from negative examples takes much work, but is rewarding. It requires us to immerse ourselves in the entire story over and over until we can see the patterns in the story which give us the inspired author's perspectives. But how better to learn God's heart than to bathe ourselves in his word?

We can often make lists of positive attributes we can learn from characters in the Bible, especially if the text specifically calls them righteous. One example of learning lessons from a character's behavior is Joseph in Matthew 1:18-25. The text specifically says that Joseph was a "righteous" person (1:19). Before listing lessons, we need to provide some background. Given the average ages of marriage among first-century Jews, Joseph was probably less than twenty and Mary was probably younger, perhaps in her mid-teens. Joseph probably did not know Mary well; sources suggest that parents did not allow Galilean couples to spend much time together before their wedding night. Also, Jewish "betrothal" was as binding legally as a marriage, hence could be ended only by divorce or the death of one partner. If the woman were charged with unfaithfulness in a court, her father would have to return to the groom the brideprice he had paid; also the groom would keep any dowry the bride had brought or was bringing into the marriage. By divorcing her privately the groom would probably forfeit such financial remuneration.

The narrative implies first of all something about commitment: Joseph was righteous even though he planned to divorce Mary, because he thought she had been unfaithful, and unfaithfulness is a very serious offense. The text also teaches us about compassion: even though Joseph believed (wrongly) that Mary had been unfaithful to him, he planned to divorce her privately to minimize her shame, thereby forgoing any monetary repayment for her misdeed and any revenge. Here Joseph's "righteousness" (1:19) includes compassion on others. The passage further emphasizes consecration: Joseph was willing to bear shame to obey God. Mary's pregnancy would bring her shame, perhaps for the rest of her life. If Joseph married her, people would assume either that he got her pregnant or, less likely, that he was a moral weakling who refused to punish her properly; in either case, Joseph was embracing Mary's long-term shame in obedience to God's will. Finally, we learn about control. In their culture, everyone assumed that a man and woman alone together could not control themselves sexually. But in their obedience to God, Joseph and Mary remained celibate even once they were married until Jesus was born, to fulfill the Scripture which promised not only a virgin conception but a virgin *birth* (1:23, 25). There are other morals in this paragraph, too (for instance, about the importance of Scripture in 1:22-23), but these are the clearest from Joseph's own life.

Now is a good opportunity to practice on one's own. One could take a passage like Mark 2:1-12 and list the sorts of morals one might draw from it. For example, one critical lesson is that the four men who brought their friend recognized that Jesus was the only answer to their need and refused to let *anything* deter them from getting to Jesus (2:4). Mark calls this determination on their part "faith" (2:5). Sometimes faith is refusing to let anything or anyone keep us from seeking Jesus for ourselves or (as in this case) for the need of a friend. Another important lesson is that Jesus responds to their faith first of all by forgiveness (2:5), because that is Christ's first priority. We may also note in passing that Jesus' true teaching generates opposition from religious professionals (2:6-7). Not everyone in religious leadership is always open to God! But while forgiveness is Christ's priority, he also is ready to grant the miracle these men sought and to demonstrate his power with signs (2:8-12). He was not a western rationalist who doubted the reality of supernatural phenomena!

One could subdivide some of these lessons and perhaps find other lessons. But one should always be careful, as noted above, to draw the *right* lessons in light of the larger context. As noted before, Jesus' popularity in the text (2:1-2) does not imply that such ministry always produces popularity, for many people ultimately asked for Jesus to be crucified (15:11-14). Nor should we read into the text something that is not clear in it; for example, we should not read into Jesus' response to "their faith" in 2:5 that the Lord will forgive others' sins because of our faith; the text nowhere indicates clearly that the man lacked faith himself. (One supposes that if he had no faith, he would have been protesting against his friends letting him down through the roof!)

Some passages do not yield as many specific applications as this passage. The story of the lepers' discovery of the abandoned Aramean tents (2 Kgs 7:3-10) functions as part of larger story about God's provision for Israel, judgment on those who doubted his prophet, and how God could replace his judgment on the nation with extraordinary mercy according to his prophetic message. At the same time, this smaller unit probably does provide some insights that also fit into the larger pattern of Scripture as a whole. God chooses not the mighty (cf. 7:2) but lepers excluded from the city (7:3) to make the discovery--desperate people who had nothing more to lose (7:4). The Bible indicates that these are often the kind of people God chooses.

Sometimes when I lead Bible studies I take a passage like Mark 2:1-12 a few verses at a time and ask people to think about the lessons in the text; this way they begin thinking how to study the Bible on their own. If their answers are too far afield, I call them back to the text; we grow more accurate as we get more practice, but we should be patient in teaching students how to read the Bible for themselves. When I taught a Sunday School class for boys ages 10-13, I would simply have them read passages of Scripture, then I would give background and we would discuss the Scripture, allowing them to discover lessons in the text. Because they knew the issues they were facing in their lives, they also could think of ways to apply those lessons to their lives far more relevant than I could have come up with on my own! After a few weeks, I told a 13-year-old that he would lead our Bible study the next week (I would simply supply cultural background). He led the discussion just as well as I would have! So did a ten-year old the next week. My point is that once we teach people how to study the Bible this way, as long as we are there to help them while they are learning, they can in turn be equipped to help others. God forbid that we should keep our learning to ourselves!

Can We Learn "Teaching" from Narratives?

Some modern theologians have been skeptical about learning "doctrine," or (literally) "teaching," from narratives. 2 Timohy 3:16 explicitly declares that all Scripture is profitable for teaching, so to rule out a teaching function for narratives altogether these theologians would have to deny that narratives are part of Scripture! But narrative makes up more of the Bible than any other genre does, and Jesus and Paul both teach from Old Testament narratives (e.g., Mk 2:25-26; 10:6-9; 1 Cor 10:1-11).[2]

If narratives did not teach, there would be no reason for different Gospels. Because Jesus did and taught so much, no one Gospel writer could have told us everything that he said or did (as Jn 21:25 explicitly points out). Rather, each Gospel writer emphasized certain points about Jesus, the way we do when we read or preach from a text in the Bible. This means that when we read Bible stories, we not only learn the historical facts about what happened, but listen to the inspired writer's *perspective* on what happened, i.e., the lessons to be drawn from the story. When the writer "preaches" to us from the stories he tells us, he

---

[2] Some of what follows below is borrowed from the appendix of my book, *3 Crucial Questions about the Holy Spirit* (Grand Rapids, MI, USA: Baker Book House, 1996).

often gives us clues for recognizing the lessons; for example, he often selects stories with a basic theme or themes that repeatedly emphasize particular lessons.

Yet despite considerable historical precedent for using biblical historical precedent, many theologians suggest that one should feel free to find in narrative only what is plainly taught in "clearer," "didactic" portions of Scripture. Although some of these scholars are among the ablest exegetes of other portions of Scripture, I must protest that their approach to Bible stories violates the most basic rules for biblical interpretation and in *practice* jeopardizes the doctrine of biblical inspiration. Did not Paul say that *all* Scripture was inspired and therefore useful for "doctrine," or teaching (2 Tim. 3:16)? I freely admit that I do not understand some portions of Scripture myself (what is the eternal function of the genealogies in Chronicles?); but other obscure parts came to make sense to me after I understood the cultural context they addressed (for instance, the design of the Tabernacle in Exodus). Some given texts are more useful for addressing common situations today than others, but *all* biblical texts have a useful function for some circumstances.

One of the most basic principles of Bible interpretation is that we should ask what the writer wanted to convey to his contemporary audience. This principle applies to narratives like the Gospels as much as to epistles like Romans. If one could simply write a "neutral" Gospel that addressed all situations universally, the Bible would undoubtedly have included it. Instead, the Bible offers us four Gospels, each selecting some different elements of Jesus' life and teachings to preach Jesus to the needs of their readers in relevant ways (which also provides us with a model for how to preach Jesus in relevant ways to our hearers). The way God chose to give us the Bible is more important than the way we wish He would have given it to us.

More importantly, we must be able to read each book first of all as a self-contained unit, because that was how God originally inspired these books. God inspired books of the Bible like Mark or Ephesians one at a time, inspiring the authors to address specific situations. The first readers of Mark could not crossreference to Ephesians or John to figure out an obscure point in Mark; they would have to read and reread Mark as a whole until they grasped the meaning of any given passage in Mark. When we read a passage in such books of the Bible, we need to read the passage in light of the total message and argument of the book as well as reading the book in light of the passages that make it up.

This is not to say that we cannot compare the results from our study of Ephesians with the results from our study of Mark. It is to say that we discount the complete character of Mark when we resort to Ephesians before we have finished our examination of Mark. For instance, the opposition Jesus faces for healing a paralytic does provide a lesson for the hostility we can expect from the world for doing God's will. The opposition to Jesus which builds in early chapters of Mark and climaxes in the cross parallels the suffering believers themselves are called to expect (8:31-38; 10:33-45; 13:9-13; 14:21-51). Mark summons Christians to endure; that Mark provides negative examples of this principle (e.g., 14:31-51) reinforces his point (even if it also shows the inadequacy of Christians to fulfill this call in our own strength).

Most cultures in the world teach lessons through stories. Most theologians who question the use of narrative, by contrast, are westerners or those trained by them, children of Enlightenment thought. In fact, not even all westerners find Bible stories inaccessible. Even in the United States, Black churches have for generations specialized in narrative preaching. In most churches children grow up loving Bible stories until they become adults and we teach them that they must now think abstractly rather than learning from concrete illustrations. Just because our traditional method of extracting doctrine from Scripture does not work well on narrative does not mean that Bible stories do not send some clear messages of their own. Instead it suggests the inadequacy of our traditional method of interpretation the way we apply it, because we are ignoring too much of God's Word.

When Jesus' followers were writing the New Testament, everyone in their culture already understood that narrative conveyed moral principles; biographers and historians expected readers to draw lessons from their examples, whether these lessons were positive or negative. Students recited such stories in regular elementary school exercises, and in more advanced levels of education learned how to apply these examples to drive home moral points.

Demanding the use of nonnarrative portions of the Bible to interpret narrative is not only disrespectful to the narrative portions; it implies a thoroughly misguided way of reading nonnarrative portions of Scripture as well. Everyone acknowledges, for instance, that Paul's letters are "occasional" documents--that is, that they address specific occasions or situations. Thus, had the Lord's Supper not been a matter of controversy in Corinth, we would know quite little about it except from Matthew, Mark, and Luke. If we then interpreted the narrative portions of Scripture only by other portions, we would assume that we do not need to observe the Lord's Supper today. Of course, Jesus provides his disciples *teaching* about the Lord's Supper within the narrative; but since the teaching is within the narrative, we can always protest that he addressed this teaching only to a select group of disciples. A few hundred years ago many Protestants explained away the Great Commission in just such a manner; today many similarly explain away the teachings of the Gospels and Acts about signs often confirming and aiding evangelism.

Not only is the traditional "doctrinal" approach inadequate for interpreting the Gospels; it is inappropriate for interpreting the epistles as well. The "narrative" way of interpreting Bible stories in fact shows us how to read the epistles properly. Paul wrote to address specific needs of churches (rarely just to send greetings); while the principles Paul employs are eternal and apply to a variety of situations, Paul expresses those principles concretely to grapple with specific situations. Before we can catch his principles, we often must recognize the situations with which he grapples; Paul's concrete words to real situations constitute case studies that show us how to address analogous situations we should address today. Paul's letters presuppose a sort of background story--he is responding to events and situations among his audience. *In other words, we must read even Paul's letters as examples.* This is how Paul read the Old Testament-- drawing theology (especially moral teaching) from its examples (1 Cor. 10:11).

I suspect that many scholars--including myself in earlier years--have felt so uncomfortable with finding theology in narrative largely because of our western academic training. In the world of the theological academy, one can feel satisfied addressing important issues like Christology while ignoring other necessary issues like domestic abuse and how to witness on a secular job. But pastors, people who do much personal witnessing and other ministers cannot ignore issues that exceed the bounds of traditional doctrinal categories. (We should not forget that those general doctrinal categories were established by Medieval theologians who often could afford to withdraw from the daily issues with which most of their contemporaries struggled. The issues they addressed were important, but they were hardly exhaustive!) I believe that the more we are forced to grapple with the same kinds of situations with which the writers of Scripture grappled, the more sensitively we will interpret the texts they wrote. When that happens, we will need to reappropriate all of Scripture for the life and faith of the Church.

One warning we need to keep in mind is that not all human actions recorded in Scripture are intended as positive examples, even when performed by generally positive characters. Scripture is realistic about human nature and openly reveals our frailties so that we can be realistic about our weaknesses and our need to depend always on God. Abraham and Sarah each laughed when they heard God's promise (Gen 17:17; 18:12-15); David almost snapped under the pressure of Saul's pursuit and Samuel's death, and thus would have slaughtered Nabal and his workers had Abigail not stopped him (1 Sam 25:32-34); despairing that anything would prove sufficient to shake Jezebel's evil control over Israel, Elijah asked to die (1 Kgs 19:4); discouraged that no one was listening to his message, Jeremiah cursed the day of his birth (Jer 20:14-18); John the Baptist doubted Jesus' identity shortly before John's execution (Lk 7:19, 23); Peter denied Jesus three times (Mk 14:72). As Paul said, we have this treasure in earthen vessels, so people may recognize that the power comes from God (2 Cor 4:7). Jesus alone exhibits no moral weaknesses, and even he identified with our being tempted (Mk 1:12-13; 14:34-42). Scripture shows the weaknesses of men and women of God so we will recognize that there are no spiritual superhumans among us--just, at best, men and women who depend on the power of God's perfect Spirit to give us victory.

Parables

Parables are a specific kind of narrative that differs somewhat from other kinds of narrative. Ancient Israelite sages in the Old Testament and in the time of Jesus used various graphic teaching forms to communicate their wisdom, forms that usually made their hearers think carefully about what they were saying. One such kind of teaching was the proverb (which we will address below). A larger category of teaching (covered by the Hebrew word *mashal*) includes proverbs, short comparisons, and sometimes more extended comparisons, including some actually intended to be allegorized (unlike most kinds of narrative in the Bible)!

By Jesus' day, Jewish teachers often communicated by telling stories in which one or two or sometimes more characters might stand for something in the real world. Often they told stories about a king who loved his son, in which the king was an analogy for God and the son for Israel. When Jesus told parables, therefore, his hearers would already be familiar with them and know how to take them.

But even though Jesus' parables sometimes were extended analogies with truths in the real world (for instance, the four different kinds of soil in the parable of the sower, Mk 4:3-20), they often included some details simply necessary for the story to make good sense, or to make it a well-told story. (This is also the case with other Jewish parables from this period.) For instance, when the Pharisee and the tax-gatherer pray in the temple (Lk 18:10), the temple does not "represent" something; that was simply the favorite place for Jerusalemites to pray. When the owner of the vineyard built a wall around his vineyard (Mk 12:1), we should not struggle to determine what the wall represents; it was simply a standard feature of vineyards, and forces the attentive reader to recognize that Jesus is alluding to the Old Testament parable in

Isaiah 5:5 so the readers will know that the vineyard represents Israel.

When we told the parable of the prodigal son earlier, the father represented God, the younger brother was an analogy for sinners and the older one for scribes and Pharisees. But the pigs do not "represent" something in particular; they merely illustrate the severity of the prodigal son's suffering and uncleanness. The prostitutes (Lk 15:30) do not represent false teaching or idolatry or anything else as if they are a standard symbol; they simply illustrate how immorally the son squandered his father's earnings.

Let us look at the parable of the Good Samaritan in Luke 10:30-35. In this parable, a man goes "down" from Jerusalem toward Jericho, when he is overtaken by robbers who beat him and leave him nearly dead. A priest and Levite pass by him, but finally a Samaritan rescues him and takes him to an inn. Augustine, a profound thinker and church father from the coast of North Africa, decided that this was the gospel story: Adam went "down" because he fell into sin, was abused by the devil, was not helped by the law but was finally saved by Christ as a good Samaritan. One could preach this interpretation and actually expect conversions, because one would be preaching the gospel. But one could preach the gospel without attaching it to this particular parable, and in fact this is not what the parable means in its context in Luke.

In Luke 10:29, a lawyer asks Jesus who is his "neighbor" that the Bible commands him to love (cf. 10:25-28). Jesus responds that his neighbor might even turn out to be a Samaritan--that real love must cross racial, tribal, even religious lines. This was probably not the answer the lawyer wanted to hear; the answer remains offensive enough even to many people today to suggest why many people would not want the parable to mean this! But why would the man go "down" from Jerusalem to Jericho? Simply because Jericho is lower in elevation than Jerusalem! Further, the road to Jericho (like many roads) hosted many robbers; a man who traveled alone would make an easy target, especially at night. The priest and Levite who passed by on the other side of the road (10:31-32) probably did so to avoid contracting ritual impurity; many Jewish teachers felt that one would become unclean for a week if even one's shadow touched a corpse, and one could not tell, unless one got close, if someone "half-dead" (10:30) were really dead or alive.

The point of the story is that some very religious people did not act very neighborly, but that a person from whom one would not expect it did so. Perhaps if we told the story today we would talk about a Sunday School teacher or minister who passed by on the other side, but a Muslim or someone from a hostile tribe rescued the person. Our hearers might react with hostility to such a comparison--but that is exactly the way Jesus' hearers would have reacted to his. The lawyer's "neighbor" might be a Samaritan. Ours might be someone we are tempted to dislike no less intensely, but Jesus commands us to love everyone.

Narratives and History

Following the influence of the Western Enlightenment, many western scholars grew skeptical of miracles hence skeptical of biblical accounts as history. Discovery after discovery from the ancient world has challenged this skepticism, new trends have begun to challenge old Enlightenment views, and today most scholars, whether Christian or not, focus more on the *meaning* of the text than its relation to history.

But the early church did expect Christian leaders to be able to respond to objections raised against the faith (2 Tim 2:25-26; Tit 1:9), so we will briefly introduce some of these issues here. Because some of my scholarly work published so far is in Gospels, I can best illustrate the methods with respect to the Gospels (whose historical reliability I affirm).

If an honest skeptic had no evidence for or against the reliability of the Gospels, should that skeptic accept or doubt the Gospels? A growing consensus of scholars is arguing that the Gospels are ancient biographies, which means that at the very least they are substantially historically reliable. They fit all the characteristics of ancient biographies and not the characteristics of other genres; thus even a skeptic should regard them as at least generally reliable.

Some nineteenth-century scholars asking historical questions noted that some parts of the Bible overlapped, such as Kings and Chronicles or Mark and Matthew. Thus they developed a method called "source history," trying to reconstruct what sources biblical writers of history used. Clearly, if they depended on earlier sources, they did not simply make things up from their imaginations. Many passages in the Bible mention their sources (Num 21:14; Josh 10:13; 2 Sam 1:18; 1 Kgs 14:19; 1 Chr 29:29; 2 Chr 27:7); 1 and 2 Chronicles cite a "Book of Kings" ten times (nine of them from 2 Chr 16 on). Although the Gospel writers write closer to the time of the events they describe, when many sources probably reported similar events, hence they do not need to name their sources, they do make it clear that many were available (Lk 1:1). Although there remains some debate, the majority scholarly view is that Matthew and Luke both used Mark and some other material they shared in common.

Beyond such a basic consensus, however, source history provided few widely accepted views. Early twentieth-century "scissors-and-paste" approaches (where skeptics chopped up Scripture to their liking) are now almost universally rejected, weakening the value of those commentaries that followed it. We also know that ancient Mediterranean storytellers drew on a wide variety of sources, including oral traditions, so we cannot always identify which report derives from which source.

Some other scholars advanced a method called "form history"; Jesus' teaching and works were reported in several different literary forms. Some of these distinct forms (such as parables) are clear, but traditional form-historians speculated too much about which forms were used by the church in particular ways, and most of their early speculations have been refuted by later scholars.

Scholars then moved to redaction-history, or editorial history. If Matthew used Mark as a source, why does Matthew edit or adapt Mark the ways that he does? Ancient biographers had complete freedom to rearrange sources and put them in their own words; a simple comparison of Matthew, Mark and Luke will indicate that they do not always follow the same sequence or use the same wording to describe the same event, and such differences are to be expected. When we find consistent patterns in Matthew's editing, we may learn about Matthew's emphases and hence what he wanted to communicate to his first audience. Some early redaction historians, however, were too confident of their abilities to reconstruct why some changes were made; later scholars have recognized that some changes were purely stylistic or for space constraints!

While there is some value in each of the above approaches, modern scholars have turned especially in two directions. The first is various forms of literary criticism, a basic component of which is usually reading each book as a whole unit to understand its meaning. The second is the social history approach, which focuses on what we have called "background." Nearly all biblical scholars today, across the entire range from "conservative" to "liberal," accept the validity of both these approaches.

2. Laws in the Bible

Biblical laws have much to teach us about justice, even if we need to take into account the culture and era of history they addressed. Thus God informs Israel that no other nation has such righteous laws as they do (Deut 4:8) and the psalmist celebrates and meditates continually on God's law (Ps 119:97).

Some laws, like the ten commandments, are stated largely as transcultural principles; it is also difficult to find genuine parallels to them in other ancient Near Eastern legal collections. Most laws, however, addressed ancient Israel as civil laws for how

Israel's society should work; these were addressed specifically to an ancient Near Eastern framework, and we need to think carefully when we look for appropriate analogies in how to apply them today.

Ancient Near Eastern law set the tone for which issues had to be addressed; Israel's laws addressed many of the same issues as Mesopotamian law. The Code of Hammurabi and other legal collections addressed ear-boring (Ex 21:6); debt-slavery (21:7); the treatment of enslaved captives (21:9); causing a miscarriage (21:22); eye for an eye and tooth for a tooth (21:23-25); negligence regarding an ox (21:28-36); brideprice (22:16-17); local responsibility for bloodguilt there (Deut 21:9-10); and so forth.

At the same time, significant differences modified ancient Near Eastern legal tradition. In other societies, one received a harsher penalty if one belonged to a lower social class; Israel's law distinctively eliminates that injustice. Whereas in Babylonian law a man who caused the death of another's daughter would have his own daughter executed, in Israelite law the man who did the killing would die. We do not know of other societies that protected ancestral lands the way Israel's laws did (Lev 25:24); this law would prevent a monopolistic accumulation of capital that would make some people wealthy at others' expense. Some offenses have more lenient penalties in Israelite law (thieves who break in during the day are executed under Babylonian law) and some have harsher penalties (Israelite law was harsher toward disobedient children). Babylonian law mandated the death penalty for those who harbored escaped slaves; God's law commanded Israel to harbor escaped slaves (Deut 23:15).

But the laws in the Old Testament, while improving the standards of their culture, do not always provide us with God's perfect *ideal* of justice. In any culture, civil laws provide a minimum standard to enable people to work together efficiently, but do not address all moral issues; for instance, a law may say, "Do not kill"; but only God can enforce the fullest implications of that law for moral standards, i.e., "You shall not *want* to kill" (Matt 5:21-26).

We may take for example the law concerning a slave who is beaten and dies in Exodus 21:20-21, where the slaveholder is not executed if the slave survives a day or two. To some extent, this follows the law for anyone who does not die immediately from injuries (21:18-19), but in this case the law specifically states that this is because the slave is the slaveholder's "property." Given what we read about slavery in Philemon and Ephesians (treated above), slavery hardly seems God's ideal purpose! Likewise, although the law condemns the sexual use of another's slave, it is condemned less harshly than adultery because she is a slave (Lev 19:20; cf. Deut 22:23).

Two centuries ago some people tried to argue from such texts that God supports slavery, but no text specifically endorses slavery. Rather, the texts address a system that already practiced slavery and made it more humane. Fellow-Israelites could not be enslaved permanently; they would serve for a time, then be set free and given capital by which they could provide for themselves (Deut 15:12-15). (Israel usually did not even meet this divine standard; cf. Jer 34:11-22.) Christians who opposed slavery cited broader biblical principles (such as loving one's neighbor as oneself, Lev 19:18; or all people being the same before God, Acts 10:28). It is this latter group of interpreters who correctly articulated the ideal of Scripture. How do we know?

When some scholars cited Deuteronomy 24 as permission for a man to divorce his wife, Jesus said that law was a "concession" to human sinfulness (Mk 10:5): that is, God did not raise the standard to its ultimate ideal because he was working within their culture. To provide workable laws in a sinful society, God limited sin rather than prohibiting it altogether. But the morality God really demands from the human heart goes beyond such concessions. God never approved of a man divorcing his wife, except for very limited reasons (Mk 10:9; Matt 19:9). Other concessions in the Old Testament may include polygamy, indentured servanthood, and perhaps holy war; God worked through or in spite of these practices, but his ideal in the New Testament is better. Ritual and civil laws may contain some moral absolutes, but they also contain concessions to the time and culture they addressed, just as Jesus recognized.

At the same time, some offenses always carried the death penalty in the Old Testament, suggesting that God took these quite seriously for all cultures: murder, sorcery, idolatry, adultery, premarital sex, homosexual intercourse, extreme rebellion against parents, and some other offenses. This does not mean that we should enforce the death penalty against all these sins today, but we should take all these offenses seriously.

In interpreting Old Testament laws, we must take into account the difference in era as well as the difference in culture. Just as people in Moses' day could not ignore God's revelation to Moses by citing the earlier revelation to Abraham, so today some things are different because of the coming of Jesus. Human nature is largely the same; God's ways of working have much in common with his ways of working in the Old Testament, but now he sometimes works in very different ways. In Moses' day, God drowned the Egyptians in the Red Sea; in Jesus' day, God unleashed a spiritual revolution that within three centuries converted much of the Roman and Axumite (East African) empires. The old covenant was good but worked by death; the new covenant works by life (2 Cor 3:6).

The law remains good and useful for ethical teaching, provided we use it properly (Rom 3:27-31; 7:12; I Tim 1:8-11). But mere obedience to the law without faith has never brought salvation; God always saved people by grace through faith (Rom 4:3-12), and since the coming of Jesus he has saved people through faith in Jesus Christ. When we consider how to apply particular details of the law today, we should also take into account other factors. Some biblical patterns, like God's command to us to rest, were given prior to the law (Gen 2:2-3; Ex 20:11), and God also gives us commands in the New Testament (Jn 13:34; Acts 2:38; I Jn 2:7-11). Also, the Spirit was quite active in the Old Testament era (I Sam 19:20-24; I Chr 25:1-2), but has become active in a new way in Christ (Jn 7:39; Acts 1:7-8; 2:17-18).

3. Biblical Prayers and Songs, especially Psalms

In some cases we have the historical context for psalms (e.g., 2 Sam 22:1 for Ps 18; 2 Sam 23:1-7), but in more cases we do not. One can gather that some psalms reflect mourning after the exile (e.g., Psalm 89, especially 89:38-51), but the context of some other psalms, say Psalm 150, is obscure--and ultimately not as necessary as with some other parts of the Bible. God inspired the psalms not only for the immediate circumstances that generated them, but for use in liturgical worship in later times (2 Chron 29:30); most resonate with many kinds of circumstances. Worship was a primary activity in the biblical temple (I Chron

6:31-32; 15:16, 28-29; 16:4-6, 41-42; 2 Chron 8:14; Ps 5:7; 18:6; 27:4; 28:2; 48:9; 63:2; 65:4; 68:24, 35; 73:17; 84:2, 10; 92:13; 96:6-8; 100:4; 115:19; 134:1-2; 135:2; 138:2; 150:1), and especially restored in periods of revival (2 Chron 20:20-24; 29:25-27; 31:2; 35:2; Ezra 3:10-11; Neh 12:24-47). The Levites praised God especially at the morning and evening sacrifices (1 Chron 23:27, 30), perhaps as part of the offering (Ps 141:2; cf. 5:3; 88:13). Such worship was usually not calm, but joyful, celebrating God's mighty works (e.g., Neh 12:27, 36, 43-46; perhaps one hundred references in the Psalms).

Israel had always used songs in worship (Ex 15:20-21), and these could be used for inspired or Spirit-directed worship (1 Sam 10:5; 2 Kings 3:15; Hab 3:19; 1 Cor 14:15); God could also use prophecy to direct the nature of worship (2 Chron 29:25). In the Spirit, a worshiper could move back and forth between speaking to God and hearing from God (2 Sam 23:1-2; Ps 46:1, 10; 91:2, 14). Most significantly, God appointed an orderly but Spirit-led worship in the temple (1 Chron 25:1-7); the New Testament develops further the importance of depending on God's Spirit to empower us for worship worthy of the Lord (Jn 4:23-24; Phil 3:3).

Psalms on the whole may be meant less to be interpreted than to be *prayed* and *sung*. Once a person is full of the psalms, they also provide models for our own spontaneous worship to God. (Because the musical and poetic culture of the ancient Near East did affect the way the Psalms were presented, we might write our psalms somewhat differently today; cf. 1 Cor 14:26; Eph 5:19. The Puritans used only the biblical psalms as their hymnbook, but we seek God to provide us contemporary songs in the music of our own cultures as well.)

Thus it is helpful for us to summarize some different kinds of psalms and their uses. Douglas Stuart, coauthor with Gordon Fee of *How to Read the Bible for All Its Worth* (Zondervan, 1993), 194-97, lists several types of psalms. We have followed and adapted much of his listing here, though they overlap and one could divide many of these categories differently. Over sixty of the psalms give individual or group examples how to express our discouragement, suffering or sorrow in prayer to God; these are often called "laments." Some Christians today think that we should never admit that we are discouraged; biblically, however, we should openly express our hurts to God. These psalms often follow a consistent structure; most include a statement of suffering, an expression of trust in God, a cry for deliverance, the assurance that God will deliver, and finally praise for God's faithfulness. Prayers like this help us deal with our suffering rather than allowing it to crush our spirit.

Thanksgiving psalms are appropriate for celebrating God's kindness to us, and are thus in some sense for different situations than laments (James 5:13);

ancient temple worshipers may have sometimes used these during thank offerings (Lev 7:7-11). Stuart lists sixteen thanksgiving psalms, some for individuals and some for God's people as a whole (Pss 18, 30, 32, 34, 40, 65-67, 75, 92, 107, 116, 118, 124, 136, 138); these normally include an introductory summary, a note of one's distress, an appeal that the psalmist made to God, a description of God's deliverance and praise for God's deliverance. In addition to these are many psalms Stuart calls "hymns of praise," which worship God without such focus on particular matters for thanksgiving (8, 19, 33, 66, 100, 103, 104, 111, 113, 114, 117, 145-50). Others emphasize trust in the Lord (11, 16, 23, 27, 62, 63, 91, 121, 125, 131).

Many psalms involve celebration and affirmation of God's works on behalf of one's people. Some psalms emphasize God's enthronement (Pss 24, 29, 47, 93, 95-99); we can use these to praise God's might and reign. Psalms that celebrate the rule of Israel's king (2, 18, 20, 21, 45, 72, 89, 101, 110, 132, 144) are useful for our celebration of our Lord and king, Jesus the Messiah; in nonroyal cultures, we need to be reminded of what it means to celebrate our Lord's rule over us. Some emphasize the holy city (46, 48, 76, 84, 87, 122), we can use these to celebrate the promised New Jerusalem and the grace God has shown us in both our future and our heritage in the holy city.

The work of the biblical historians, prophets, and sages is compatible with psalms as well. Some psalms celebrate God's work in our heritage in Israel's history (78, 105, 106, 135, 136); some sound like the messages of the prophets, including a covenant lawsuit summoning God's people to obedience (Ps 50); some are wisdom psalms, sounding like the teaching of the sages (1, 36, 37, 49, 73, 112, 119, 127, 128, 133). We can teach and learn through our worship (Col 3:16).

Psalms can also express our passionate devotion to God, a devotion that we confess based not always on feeling but which we reaffirm in the very act of confessing it. When we sing to God that he matters to us more than anything else, we reaffirm our devotion to him (e.g., Ps 42, 63).

The psalms provide ways for us to express anguish, sorrow, hope, despair, and joy in prayer to God. Some psalms are for mild distress; others, that end on a note of despair (Ps 89:49-51) are encouraging only to the person who is in great despair and needs to express his or her pain fully to God. Even though we know that God ultimately will deliver us--in life or in death--we need to express our feelings before him. Imprecatory psalms, such as Ps 137 (announcing blessing for one who kills the babies of Babylon as Babylon has done with Israel's babies), fall into this category (see also Pss 12, 35, 58, 59, 69, 70, 83, 109, 140). Instead of pressing the literal meaning as far as possible, we should consider the rhetorical function of these psalms: they are prayers for swift vindication of the oppressed, for God to act with justice quickly. The oppressed does not take vengeance for himself or herself, but cries out for vindication the way Abel's blood did (Gen 4:10; Matt 23:35; Lk 11:51; Heb 11:4; 12:24). This practice also appears in the New Testament (Rev 6:10; cf. 2 Tim 4:14), though Jesus wants us ultimately to forgive and love so fully that we pray good for our enemies (Matt 5:44; Lk 6:28).

This approach to the psalms is not a way to get around texts uncomfortable for those of us conditioned differently by Jesus' teaching. We are trying to read the psalms according to their intention, thus according to their rhetorical function. Thus some psalms sound as if God always grants blessing to the righteous, whereas others note the frequent distresses of the righteous. Yet both psalms are in the same psalter, because those who first wrote and sang the psalms saw no contradiction; they used the psalms to express their hearts before God, and God inspired their worship and was pleased with it.

Psalms thus can include summons to worship, building to a crescendo of emotion. ("Hallelujah," meaning "Praise the Lord!" literally is a command to praise the Lord rather than a word of praise itself; Levite musicians prophesied to the people as they led them in worship--1 Chron 25:1-2.) Other psalms can be inspired laments, providing acceptable models for us expressing our grief. Others are prayers for vindication. Although we are to pray kind things for our enemies (Lk 6:28), prayers for vindication continue in the New Testament era (Rev 6:10; cf. 2 Tim 4:14), as we have noted.

Psalms are mainly meant to be prayed, but we can also preach and teach from them provided we recognize that we are teaching models for various kinds of prayer. For instance, Psalm 150 tells us where to praise God--both in his sanctuary and in heaven, i.e., everywhere (150:1; Hebrew often summarized the whole by contrasting opposite parts); why we should praise God--both for what he has done and for who he is (150:2); how we should praise God--with dancing and all available instruments (150:3-5); and finally, who should praise God--anyone with breath (150:6). The Psalms also can provide other encouragements. For example, Psalm 2 predicts the victory of Israel's king over the nations who mock him. This reminds us that ultimately it is not people in our society or other societies that wield power over us; God is in control, and he will reveal that; no human empire that rebels against him has ever endured and none ever will.

4. Proverbs

Wisdom teachers, or sages, often taught in easily memorizable sayings called proverbs. Most cultures have some familiarity with this genre; Americans have sayings like, "Haste makes waste," and traditional African societies have made much more abundant use of proverbs.

Proverbs are short, succint statements of general principle. As such, they are summaries of what is normal, not unconditional promises for all circumstances. Some general principles may actually conflict with one another in practice in specific situations. Thus in Proverbs 26:4-5 one should both answer a fool according to his folly, and not answer a fool according to his folly. For his sake you should correct him; for your sake you should be careful not to become like him. Both are true principles, and recognizing both requires us to keep attentive to the breadth of Scripture, rather than taking one text and reading it into all others without first considering the meaning of each text.

One who preaches from Proverbs may wish to gather different proverbs on the same topic and preach them together. This is important because most of the Book of Proverbs consists of sayings in random order, so normal rules of context do not apply. But the broader context of genre does apply, and pulling together other wisdom-sayings on the same topic can be very helpful.

By ignoring the genre of Proverbs, some have used isolated proverbs as unconditional promises which they may then "claim" with certainty. (Some, like Job's friends, therefore use Proverbs' general principles about success for the righteous to condemn as lacking in faith those who do not experience such success. This approach completely misunderstands the nature of proverbs.) Some have also come up with strange doctrines by taking individual proverbs out of the context of the larger collection of sayings on the same subject.

For example, some say that we can speak things into existence based on some proverbs (as well as some other texts out of context). They note that the tongue can bring death or life, hurt or healing (Prov 18:21; 12:18). But when one compares other proverbs about the tongue bringing healing or life, their meaning becomes clear: you can edify or hurt others by your speech, and you can get yourself into trouble or help yourself by how you speak to others (Prov 12:14; 13:2-3; 18:20; 21:23). Other statements in Proverbs about healing include the well-being of those who choose trustworthy messengers (Prov 13:17), have tranquil or joyful hearts (14:30; 17:22), receive good news (25:25) or hear encouraging words (16:24). Many texts emphasize the therapeutic value of the tongue, especially in relationships (12:25; 15:1, 4, 23; 25:11-12, 25). Egyptians and Mesopotamians also had proverbs about the tongue and about words bringing healing or death, not in the sense of speaking things into existence but in the sense of getting one in trouble or out of it (see, e.g., the "Words of Ahiqar").

We should also note the "rhetorical function" of proverbs. Ancient sages offered proverbs in short, succinct statements as general principles. Proverbs were poetry (often with the second line contrasting with the first line), and they were short summaries that would not list all possible exceptions to the principles they articulated. They might use humor, hyperbole (rhetorical overstatement), irony, and other means to communicate graphically; proverbs were intended to be memorable and practical, not detailed statements of philosophy and certainly not legal guarantees. We must read them according to the character in which they were written.

We briefly mention some other kinds of wisdom literature. Job and Ecclesiastes both challenge the kind of conventional wisdom in Proverbs: What happens when the righteous suffer and the wicked prosper? That the Bible includes these books reminds us that the general principles in Proverbs are principles only, not ironclad guarantees that we can "claim" as if God is obligated to answer them. (He does, however, often answer our prayers of faith, including faith strengthened by such principles. But that is a different matter.) That the Bible also includes such a wide range of perspectives (although not contradictions) also may warn us to keep our own boundaries wide: God may send many Christians to us with different kinds of wisdom, and we should have the wisdom to embrace all kinds of wisdom. We may meet those who tend to be cautious and skeptical (like the cynicism of Ecclesiastes), those who have learned through the sufferings of Job, and those who have seen general principles of God's faithfulness to the righteous; we should welcome them all, and help them to work together in Christ's one body, just as different books of the Bible work together in one canon.

5. Romance Literature

Although some psalms may have been used at royal weddings (Ps 45), the largest continuous piece of romance literature in the Bible is the Song of Solomon. Through history many interpreters were annoyed that sacred Scripture would devote such attention to so "secular"a topic as marital romance, and so interpreted the song allegorically concerning the relationship between God and Israel or Christ and the church. But the song makes better sense in its literal meaning (Christ's marriage to the church has some parallels to human romance, but the probable allusions to intercourse, a marital disagreement, and jealousy do not fit that interpretation!)

God gave us this song in our Bible because he values marital romance highly and wants husbands and wives to enjoy their love for each other. Some of the romance language that is unfamiliar to us was standard romance language in its day (for instance, Egyptian love songs also celebrate as a romantic setting the coming of spring and the voice of animals emerging at that time--cf. Song 2:12).

The Song deals with many practical aspects of marital romance (through the specific example of the king and his bride): for example, he affirms her beauty (1:9-10, 15; 2:2; 4:1-15); she affirms his attractiveness (1:16; 2:3; 5:10-16); they participate in the wedding banquet (2:4); they experience a misunderstanding and are reconciled (5:2-8); one should beware of provoking jealousy (8:6).

This book is useful for marriage counseling and for preaching about marriage. Only after we have internalized its lessons for our own marriages should we find some marriage principles in the song that also apply to our relationship with our Lord.

6. Jesus' Teachings

Jesus' teachings are not a broad genre like poetry or narrative; in fact, they mix together elements of different kinds of genres. Jesus was, among other things, a Jewish sage, so he often uses the teaching style used by Jewish teachers in his day: for example, rhetorical overstatements, wisdom proverbs (see above), and parables. At the same time, Jesus was a prophet, and sometimes gave oracles like prophets did ("Woe to you, Capernaum...!") Of course, as the Messiah, Jesus was more than a prophet or a sage, and he often spoke with greater authority than either prophets or sages did. But he also used many teaching techniques that were familiar to his people in his day.

For our example, we will take Jesus' teaching on divorce. Many people assume that what Jesus said on a particular occasion covers every situation, but while that is often the case, sometimes Jesus himself provided different perspectives for different kinds of situations. Thus we recognize that while Jesus wants us to love him more than our parents, we "hate" them only by comparison with our love for him (Lk 14:26); elsewhere he instructs us to provide for them in their old age (Mk 7:10-13).

Some people quote only Jesus' saying that remarriage is adultery (Mk 10:11-12; Lk 16:18), but what kind of saying is this? When Jesus says that one who lusts should pluck out his eye to avoid hell (Matt 5:28-30), should we take more literally his saying about remarriage that occurs immediately afterward (Matt 5:31-32)? The only way to test this is to examine it in the context of all of Jesus' teachings on the subject.

First we should examine the "why" of Jesus' teaching, as best as possible. In Jesus' day the Pharisees debated among themselves as to the grounds for a husband to divorce his wife; the stricter school said a man could divorce his wife if she were unfaithful to him, but the more lenient school said he could divorce his wife if she burned his bread. In Jewish Palestine (as opposed to Roman laws), husbands could divorce their wives for almost any reason; wives could not divorce their husbands or prevent themselves from being divorced. Jesus was at least in part defending an innocent party from being wronged: the husband who divorces his wife and remarries commits adultery "against her"--against his wife (Mk 10:11). This was a sin not only against God, but also against another person innocent of the divorce (cf. also Mal 2:14).

Second we should examine what this saying literally claims. "Adultery" in the literal sense is being unfaithful to one's marriage partner; for remarriage to be adultery against a former spouse means that, in God's sight, one is still married to one's former spouse. If we take this literally, this means that marriage cannot be dissolved, and that Christians should break up all second and third marriages. (Interestingly, despite the scandal this would have caused in ancient society, we have no record of anyone breaking up later marriages in the New Testament.) But is this a literal statement, or one of Jesus' deliberate overstatements meant to grab people's attention--like plucking out the eye, a camel passing through a needle's eye, or a mustard seed of faith? We can easily answer this question by examining Jesus' other sayings on the same subject.

In the same context as Mark 10:11, Jesus also says, "What God joined together, let no one separate" (Mk 10:9). In 10:11, marriage cannot be broken; in 10:9, it should not be and must not be, but it is breakable. The difference in meaning here is this: one says that one is always married to one's first spouse; the other says that one should remain married to one's first spouse. The one is a statement; the other is a demand. Yet marriage cannot be both unbreakable and breakable; so it is possible that 10:11 is a deliberate overstatement (hyperbole) whereas 10:9 communicates its real intention: to keep us from divorcing, not to break up new marriages.

Other sayings of Jesus help us further. For instance, Jesus himself did not take Mk 10:11 literally: he regarded the Samaritan woman as married five times, not as married once and committing only adultery thereafter (Jn 4:18). Further, Jesus himself allows an exception in two of the four passages where he addresses divorce. A follower of Christ must not break up their marriage, but if their spouse breaks it up by sexual unfaithfulness, Jesus does not punish the innocent person (Matt 5:32; 19:9). In that case, the marriage may be broken, but only one person is guilty of breaking it. (Because both Jewish and Roman law required divorce for adultery, Mark and Luke could assume this exception without having to state it explicitly.) When Paul quotes Jesus' prohibition of divorce, he tells Christians not to divorce their spouses, whether or not the spouses are Christian (1 Cor 7:10-14). But if the spouse leaves, the Christian is not held responsible for the spouse's behavior (1 Cor 7:15). His wording, "not under bondage," "not bound" (7:15), is the very language used in ancient Jewish divorce contracts for freedom to remarry. Paul therefore applies Jesus' teaching as a demand for faithfulness to marriage, not a statement about breaking up marriages: Christians must never break up their own marriages, but if the marriage is broken against their will, we must not punish them, either. Jesus spoke to defend an innocent spouse, not to make their condition more difficult!

But even though Jesus is not really calling Christians to break up remarriages, this does not mean we should not take seriously what he is saying. The point of a deliberate overstatement is not to let us say, "Oh, that is just overstatement; we may ignore it." The point of overstatement is to grab our attention, to force us to consider how serious is his demand. Genuine repentance (expressed in restitution) cancels past sins, but one cannot premeditate sin and expect one's repentance to be genuine. Christians are not held responsible for marriages broken against their wills, but they are responsible before God to do everything genuinely in their power to make their marriages work. In this example, we have tried to show how we need to listen carefully to why Jesus speaks certain ways, and to examine all of his teachings to discern when he speaks literally and when he overstates his point parabolically. But overstatements are not meant to be ignored; they are meant to grip our attention all the more! We should also add two words of caution: Jesus himself uses principles like "compassion rather than sacrifice" (Matt 9:13; 12:7) and looking for the heart of the message (Matt 5:21-22; 23:23-24). But also we should be honest in grappling with what he says: proper fear of God will give us integrity in searching for truth rather than trying to justify how we want to live (cf. Prov 1:7).

7. Gospels

The Gospels are a specific kind of narrative, but rather than treating them only as narrative we make some special points here. The Gospels fit the format of ancient biographies. (Some early twentieth century scholars disputed this premise, but more recent scholarship has increasingly returned to the historic view that the Gospels are ancient biographies.)

Ancient biographers followed some fairly standard conventions in their writing, but some of these differed from the ways we write biographies today. For example, ancient biographies sometimes started with their subject's adulthood (as in Mark or John) and sometimes arranged their story in topical more than chronological order (so, for example, Matthew's reports of Jesus' teaching; that is why events are not always in the same order from one Gospel to another). Nevertheless, biographers were not free to make up new stories about their heroes; they could choose which stories to report and put them in their own words, but other writers criticized those who made stories up. Further, one need not quote people verbatim, though one did have to get correct the sense of what they meant. Knowing such details about various kinds of ancient narratives helps us be even more precise when we learn principles for interpreting narratives. (We can also identify other kinds of narratives in the Bible more specifically than we have; for example, the Book of Acts is a special kind of history book that was common in the first century.)

Here we offer just a few comments on the historical trustworthiness of the Gospels as ancient biographies, using Luke 1:1-4 as a simple outline. We know from Luke 1:1 that by the time that Luke wrote, many written sources (other Gospels) were already in circulation. (Most of those Gospels no longer exist. Apart from the Gospels in the New Testament, all first-century Gospels have been lost. The so-called "Lost Gospels" some people speak about are forgeries, novels, or sayings-collections from later eras.) Luke himself writes in the lifetime of some of the apostles, and already many others have written before him! People were writing Gospels when others still remembered Jesus' teachings very accurately.

Further, there were many oral stories about Jesus being passed on that went back to the eyewitnesses (Lk 1:2). Many African societies have members of the tribe (in some places called a griot) who can recall centuries of information that matches well with written records of European travelers. Ancient Mediterranean people were excellent with memory. Schoolchildren learned by rote memorization, focusing on sayings of famous teachers. Orators regularly memorized speeches that were hours in length. Teachers expected their students, their disciples, to memorize and propagate their teachings--that was the main duty of disciples. Students regularly took notes, and often ancient teachers attest that students reported their teachings exactly as the teachers gave them (for documentation, see the introduction in Craig Keener, *Matthew* [InterVarsity, 1996], or the more detailed volume I wrote for Eerdmans). It is actually historically naive to doubt that Jesus' disciples accurately passed on his teachings; that was precisely what ancient disciples were for!

Further, we can trust the testimony of these eyewitnesses. The apostles remained in positions of leadership in the early church; both Acts and Paul mention Jesus' brother and the leading apostles in Jerusalem. (No one had any reason to invent such people, and the spread of Christianity started somewhere; further, diverse sources attest them. So virtually no one today denies their existence.) Because of their leadership, no one could make up stories about Jesus that contradicted their true reports about Jesus. Further, no one can accuse them of lying about Jesus. They were so convinced that they spoke truth about him that they were prepared to die for their claims. Moreover, they were not simply dying for what they believed; they were dying for what they saw and heard when they were with him.

Third, Luke had the opportunity to investigate their claims (Lk 1:3, according to the Greek and most translations). Back when it was still possible to do so, Luke verified his sources by interviewing witnesses, wherever possible. Some sections of Acts say "we" because Luke was traveling with Paul at those points, and those sections include their journey to Jerusalem and Palestine, where they remained two years (Acts 21:15-17; 24:27; 27:1). That gave him the opportunity to interview Jesus' younger brother James, among others (Acts 21:18).

Finally, Luke himself would not be able to make these stories up. He is confirming accounts for Theophilus, not introducing new ones (Lk 1:4). That is, while some eyewitnesses are still alive, the stories Luke records were already known by Theophilus. This further confirms to us that, even on purely historical grounds, the Gospels are trustworthy. (In the same way, Paul can remind his readers of miracles they themselves have witnessed, often through his ministry, or mention that other witnesses of the risen Christ are still alive and hence available for interview: 1 Cor 15:6; 2 Cor 12:12; Gal 3:5.)

8. Letters

As we read letters in the Bible, we must read them first of all as letters addressed to real people in the writer's own day, for this is what they explicitly claim to be (e.g., Rom 1:7). Only after we have understood the letters in their own historical context can we consider how to rightly apply them to our situations today. In contrast to those who assume that letters require less interpretation than other parts of Scripture, they are actually among the parts of Scripture *most* closely tied to their historical situation.

For example, how does one apply the teachings of 1 Corinthians in a very different cultural setting? The promise of future resurrection (1 Cor 15) seems easy enough. More controversially in many cultures, in many churches in many parts of the world it is taken for granted that women must wear head coverings (1 Cor 11:2-16), even if that is no longer part of the broader culture. But what about food offered to idols (1 Cor 8-10)? In cultures where people no longer sacrifice food to idols, like much of the western world, are we free to simply skip over those chapters? Or are there transcultural principles that Paul uses there which would also be relevant to other cultures?

As we noted in more detail above, cultural background in Bible study is not optional; we must take the original situation into account to fully understand the Bible. This is at least as true of letters as it is of every other part of the Bible, and maybe more so, because letters explicitly address specific congregations or people facing specific situations. Some passages are difficult to understand because the original audience already knew what was being addressed, and we are not always able to reconstruct it (2 Thess 2:5); in such cases we must learn humility! After all, if Paul was with the Corinthians for eighteen months (Acts 18:11), one might expect him to allude to some issues with them that we know little about (1 Cor 1:16; 3:4-6; 15:29). But even in such cases we can often catch the general point of the passage as a whole, and that is what we need most. Further research into the background usually reveals more details, but there will always be some things we do not know until Jesus returns (1 Cor 13:12).

Writers of biblical letters often followed standards of "rhetoric," proper speaking and writing conventions of their day. Knowing some of those customs can help us understand the letters better (for instance, why Paul often opens with "grace and peace be with you, from God and Christ," which links Christ as deity alongside the Father). At the same time, those writers were not simply showing off their writing abilities. They were making points, correcting problems and encouraging Christians in particular situations. Once we understand the situation, we can usually understand how the writer is addressing that situation. These writers applied eternal principles to concrete situations in their own day; to allow for an equivalent impact, we must reapply those principles to the concrete situations of our day, taking into account the differences in culture.

When we apply them, we must make sure that we find the appropriate analogies between the situations Paul addresses and our situations today. For example, some interpreters believe that Paul prohibits most women in one congregation from teaching because they were generally uneducated, hence could prove easily misled (1 Tim 2:11-12). In that culture, his command that they should "learn" (2:11; "quietly and submissively" was the appropriate way for all novices to learn) actually liberated women, who normally did not receive direct instruction except by sitting in services. It makes a difference whether or not this is the issue: if not, the appropriate analogy today may be that women should never teach the Bible (though this would leave in question what to do with other texts, like Rom 16:1-2, 7; Phil 4:2-3; Judg 4:4; 1 Cor 11:4-5). If so, the analogy today may be that unlearned people, whether male or female, should not teach the Bible.

Gordon Fee, in one of his chapters on "Epistles" in his book coauthored with Doug Stuart, *How to Read the Bible for All Its Worth* (Zondervan, 1993), sugests two main general principles for interpreting letters. First, "a text cannot mean what it never could have meant to its author or his or her readers" (p. 64). He notes for instance that one cannot argue that the "perfect" in 1 Corinthians 13:10 refers to the completion of the New Testament--since Paul's readers had no way of knowing that there would be a New Testament. Second, "Whenever we share comparable particulars (i.e., similar specific life situations) with the first-century setting, God's Word to us is the same as his Word to them" (p. 65). Murmuring, complaining, sexual immorality and greed will always be wrong, no matter how much or little any culture practices them.

What do we do with texts that address situations very much unlike our situations today? Jewish and Gentile Christians divided over food laws and holy days, and Paul warned them in Romans 14 not to divide over such secondary matters. If we are in circles where we do not know any Christians who keep Old Testament festivals and who abstain from pork, do we simply skip over this chapter? Yet Paul's advice in this chapter works from a broader principle in addressing the specific situation. The principle is that we should not divide from one another over secondary issues, issues that are not at the heart of the gospel and Christian morality.

Paul wrote to specific, real-life congregations. Because he was not expecting Christians for many centuries later to keep reading his letters in different cultures and situations (cf. Mk 13:32), he did not stop to distinguish for us his transcultural principles on which he based his advice from the concrete advice he gave to these congregations in their situations. Fee lists several principles for distinguishing transcultural principles from the specific examples the Bible gives us, the most important of which we have adapted here. First, we should look for the "core," or the transcultural principle in the text. This is important so we keep the emphasis on Christ's gospel and do not become legalists on details like some of Jesus' enemies were. Second, the Bible presents some matters as transcultural moral norms, such as in Paul's vice lists (Rom 1:28-31; 1 Cor 6:9-10). But in different cultures the Bible allowed different customs in terms of women's work outside the home (Prov 31:16, 24; 1 Tim 5:14) or various forms of ministry (Judg 4:4; Phil 4:3; 1 Tim 2:12). If different passages allow different practices, we see these practices as providing guidelines in a specific culture, but not a transcultural principle behind them without exceptions.

Third, we need to understand the cultural options available to the writer. For example, biblical writers wrote in an era where no one was trying to abolish slavery; that the Bible's writers do not explicitly address an issue that no one had raised does not suggest that they would have side with slavery's supporters had the question been raised! On the other hand, Greeks in Paul's day held various views regarding premarital sex, homosexual intercourse, and so on, but the Bible is unanimous in condemning such practices. Fourth, we need to take into account differences in situation: in the first century, men were far more apt to be educated, including in the Bible, than women; would Paul have written exactly the same applications for today, when women and men are more likely to share equal opportunities for education? Fee's principles resemble those we articulated above on the use of cultural background.

We may provide one stark example of how we need to take Paul's situation into account. In two texts, Paul requires women to keep "silence" in church (1 Cor 14:34-35; 1 Tim 2:12). If we press this to mean all that it could mean, women should not even sing in church! Few churches today press these verses this far, but are they ignoring the passages' meaning? Not necessarily. In other texts, Paul commends women for their labors for the kingdom (Phil 4:2-3), and in Romans 16 commends more women for their services than men (even though he mentions more men!) Moreover, he at least occasionally uses his most common terms for his male fellow workers to some women: "fellow worker" (Prisca, Rom 16:3); *diakonos* ("servant," Phoebe, Rom 16:1); and once even "apostle" (Junia, according to the best translations; Rom 16:7)! Even more importantly, he accepts women praying and prophesying with their heads covered (1 Cor 11:4-5). How can they pray and prophesy if later in the same letter he requires them to be completely silent in church (1 Cor 14:34-35)? Does the Bible contradict itself here? Did Paul contradict himself in the very same letter?

But the two texts about silence probably do not address all kinds of silence, but deal with special kinds of situations. The only kind of speech specifically addressed in 1 Corinthians 14:34-35 is asking questions (14:35). It was common for people to interrupt teachers and lecturers with questions in Jewish and Greek cultures alike; but it was rude for unlearned people to do so, and they might have considered it especially rude for unlearned women. Keep in mind that women were usually much less educated than men; in Jewish culture, in fact, boys were taught to recite God's law but girls almost never received this education. As to 1 Timothy 2:11-12, scholars still debate how Paul uses the Old Testament background (he applies Old Testament examples different ways in different passages, even the example of Eve: 2 Cor 11:3). But one point, at least, is interesting: Paul's letters to Timothy in Ephesus are the only letters in the entire Bible where we know that false teachers were specifically targeting women with their false teachings (2 Tim 3:6). In fact, they may have targeted widows (1 Tim 5:9) who owned homes so they could use their houses for churches--one of the Greek terms in 1 Tim 5:13 nearly always meant spreading "nonsense" or false ideas. Those who knew less about the Bible were naturally most susceptible to false teachings; those who do not know the Bible should not be allowed to teach it. Whatever other conclusions one may draw from this, it seems unlikely that Paul would have refused to let women sing in church!

But Fee also cautions against extending the application too far beyond the point in the text. If the law is summed up in love (Rom 13:8-10), we apply the text rightly to love our neighbor as ourselves, a principle which has a potentially infinite number of applications. But some people have taught as if this principle empties all the moral content of the law, so that adultery or bank robbery are fine as long as one is motivated by love. That such an application twists the meaning of the text is obvious, but we practice other such distortions all the time. For instance, we sometimes quote 1 Corinthians 3:16, "you are a temple of God," and use this against smoking, because smoking is bad for your body. The text in context, however, means that we as a church are God's temple and dwelling-place (3:9-15), and anyone who defiles that temple by causing division incurs God's judgment (3:17). This text applies even to nonsmoking Christians to the extent that we are unloving toward other Christians! A little better would be 1 Corinthians 6:19, "your body is the temple of the Holy Spirit." This verse refers to our individual body, which should be used for the Lord only (6:20). Paul's own primary point, however, is that our bodies should not be joined to prostitutes (6:15-17). This is a text to be used against sexual immorality! If we try to apply the principle also to smoking, because that is not glorifying God with our bodies, then we should also apply it to gluttony, lack of exercise, poor nutrition, and other problems damaging to our bodies. Our extension of Paul's principle in this verse may be legitimate, but it is certainly secondary to Paul's own focus, and Paul's own focus should be primary to us: if we are joined to Christ, we must avoid sexual immorality.

Different letters were written in different ways, but for the most part we need to read letters carefully in sequence and the entire way through. Romans develops an argument through the entire book (as noted above); 1 Corinthians takes on several related issues, but most of those issues take up many paragraphs through several chapters (1 Cor 1-4, the church divided especially over the most skilled speakers; 1 Cor 5-7, mainly sexual issues; 1 Cor 8-11, mainly food issues; 1 Cor 12-14, spiritual gifts). You might practice discerning that argument by thinking up titles for each paragraph and show how these paragraphs relate to one another, developing a continuous argument.

We provide here a summary of our guidelines for understanding and reapplying (contextualizing) the Bible's letters:

Distinguishing principles from applications; reapplying (recontextualizing).

(1) Read first as letters addressed to real people
(2) Learn the situation; how does writer address situation?
   a. What is the culture and (as best as we can tell) the specific situation he addresses?
   b. Rhetorical criticism: are there cultural reasons for why he constructs his argument in a particular format?
   c. Determine how he addresses the situation (agreeing, disagreeing, a mixture of both elements, etc.)
(3) Is his application transcultural, or is what is transcultural merely the principle behind this application?
   a. In different cultures or situations, does the Bible present alternative teachings?
   b. Does the writer agree or disagree with majority views in his culture?
   c. If he agrees on some points, he *may* be embracing morally neutral elements of his culture for the sake of relating to it positively.
   d. If he disagrees on some points (or if he takes a firm position and his culture holds diverse

views), he is likely articulating a transcultural norm.

(4) For equivalent impact, we must apply principle to equivalent situations today.

  a. What situations today are almost exact analogies to those of the first audience?
  b. What situations today (in our lives, others' lives, society, etc.) are similar to the original situation in various respects?
  c. What other situations might the principle address (provided we have correctly ascertained the principle behind the application)?
  d. Make sure your application fits the kind the original writer would have given; if he had lived in our day, what would he have said to this situation?

9. Prophecy

Many prophecies appear in the Bible's historical books, but we also have books that consist primarily of prophecy with merely some historical summaries in them, such as Isaiah, Jeremiah, Ezekiel, or Hosea or Nahum. In the historical books, it is usually clear when prophecies address a specific king or period in Israel's history, in which case we study them the way we study God's other actions in historical narrative (see discussion above.) But how do we interpret books of prophecies that do not provide the full background concerning the situations they address? Below we provide some principles that should prove helpful.

(1) Find out who and what circumstances the prophecy addresses in context.

To ascertain the circumstances prophecies addressed, you can usually discover the specific era in which a prophet prophesied by looking at the beginning of the book, which usually (though not always) lists the reigns of the rulers during which the prophet prophesied. Then you can turn to 1-2 Kings and 1-2 Chronicles to learn what was going on in Israel in that period of time.

(2) Use the law and earlier prophets as background.

The prophets saw themselves as calling Israel back to the covenant; many judgments they announce simply fulfill the warnings of curses in Deuteronomy 27-28. Their language regularly echoes and recycles the language of earlier prophets for their own generation. Many of the prophets repeat the same basic message over and over, except in creatively new, poetic ways. Some surrounding cultures claimed prophets, but none of them had a succession of prophets with the same basic message generation after generation. (The city of Mari had prophets whose most "moral" reproof to a king might be that he was in danger of losing a battle because he was not paying enough money to the temple. Egypt had prophetic writers who denounced injustices of past rulers, which is a little closer but still not like the Bible's prophetic succession.)

(3) Before the exile, prophets usually prophesied in poetry in their books.

That prophets often prophesied in poetry invites us to interpret them in a particular manner. First, most ancient poetry was rich in symbolism, worded so as to capture attention. Most people knew that not all the details were literal; rather, one should strive to catch the basic point. Some details were even deliberately obscure until their fulfilment, though clear enough in retrospect that one would recognize both God's wisdom and humanity's foolishness in not understanding it.

Second, Israelite prophecy involved parallelism, as in the psalms and proverbs. (When the King James was translated, this principle was not recognized, but nearly all newer translations arrange biblical prophecies in lines like other poetry, which makes it easy to recognize the poetic form.) Some modern poetry and songs balance sound, for instance, by rhyme and rhythm; but the Israelites balanced especially ideas. Thus the second line might repeat the thought of the first line (either in the same words or in similar ones that might slightly develop the thought). Or the second line might give the opposite point (e.g., if the first line says, the memory of the righteous will be blessed, the second might note that the name of the wicked will rot). In such cases, we should not read into parallel lines different thoughts. Some preachers have even taken separate points of their sermon from parallel lines, but in the original poetry, these separate lines were not separate ideas; they were simply varied ways of stating the same idea.

(4) Was the prophecy fulfilled already? Does some remain?

Here you should check historical parts of Bible and other historical information to see if a prophecy was fulfilled. Often prophecies are poetic ways to give the general sense, while the particular application remains ambiguous (Is 37:29, 33-37); God does not give prophecy to satisfy our curiosity, but to tell us just what we need. Thus we should not expect literal fulfilment of every detail as if prophecies were prose rather than poetry (although God sometimes did fulfill details literally). Thus, for example, all scholars agree that Jeremiah prophesied before Jerusalem's fall, announcing in advance judgment on his own people. (This was unusual in the ancient Near East, where prophets were often expected to be patriotic and encourage their people to victories.) But Jeremiah (and Deuteronomy) prophesied the restoration of Israel to the land. When the Assyrians had carried people into captivity, no one ever returned, and no one expected matters to be different with the Babylonians. But a generation after Jeremiah's death the Judean exiles returned to their land. This was a remarkable, large-scale fulfilment, not naturally expected and not able to be viewed as coincidence, that validates Jeremiah's prophecy even if some details were intended poetically. Jeremiah's very writing style lets us know that many of his details are merely poetic, graphic ways of communicating his broader point (e.g., Jer 4:7-9, 20-31). (Parts of Daniel include more details in prose; these occurred exactly as Daniel predicted them.)

A few prophecies were never fulfilled and never will be (e.g., Jer 46:13; Ezek 29:19; 30:10), because people responded to the threats or took for granted the promises; God gives many prophecies in a conditional manner (Jer 18:7-10).

Of prophecies that were fulfilled, part may remain future. This is because there are consistent patterns in God's dealing with humanity, because both God and human nature have remained the same. Thus, for example, the temple was repeatedly judged in "abominations of desolation," by the Babylonians (587 BC), by Antiochus Epiphanes (second century BC), by Pompey (first century BC), by Titus (first century AD) and by Hadrian (second century AD). (Referring in advance to Titus' destruction of the temple, Jesus could speak of an abomination of desolation within one generation--Matt 23:36-38; 24:1-3, 15, 34--which was fulfilled forty years after Jesus predicted it.) Because there are many evil emperors in history, the "mystery of lawlessness is already at work" (2 Thess 2:7); because deceivers remain, there are already many antichrists (1 Jn 2:18).

When a prophecy was not fulfilled but deals with God's unconditional promises, how much of it remains future? For example, the Israelites' return from Babylon was a clear miracle, although Cyrus needed less miraculous persuasion to let his captives return home than Pharaoh had needed when the Israelites had been slaves in Egypt. (Indeed, he sent home other captive peoples as well.) But Isaiah's exalted prophecies of the deserts blossoming with lilies were not fulfilled; Israel remained a very small kingdom. (This disappointment seemed no less severe than the generation that wandered in the wilderness after a miraculous deliverance from slavery in Egypt.) Some aspects of Isaiah's prophecy were fulfilled in Jesus' ministry, both physically and spiritually (e.g., Is 35:5-6; 61:1-2; Matt 11:5; Lk 4:18-19). But history also suggests that God is preserving Israel for a purpose. Israel was scattered again a generation after Jesus' crucifixion, as he warned would happen in judgment (Lk 21:20-24). Yet the Jewish people never disappeared, in contrast to the Hittites, Edomites, Philistines and other nations that were assimilated into other peoples.

Jesus' coming may appear at first sight a less dramatic deliverance than the first exodus or the return from Babylon, but within a few centuries Judea's oppressors were converted to belief in Israel's

God--something more dramatic than happened with Pharaoh or Cyrus. Today perhaps half the world's population acknowledges that there is one God; much of this faith may be inadequate in many respects, but from the standpoint of Jeremiah's or Jesus' day it would appear an amazing miracle. All this leads us to expect the fulfilment of future promises of restoration, though we cannot get past the prophets' symbolic language to fathom all the details. Those who have been grafted into the biblical heritage and hope by faith (Rom 2:26-29; 11:17-24) share in those future promises.

We must be careful, however, in speaking of "double fulfilments." Many of the "secondary fulfilments" of Scripture we see in the New Testament are actually applications or analogies with the Old Testament, not claims to primary fulfilment. Thus, for example, when Hosea said, "Out of Egypt have I called my son," the context makes clear that he speaks of Israel in the exodus (Hos 11:1). When Matthew applies this to Jesus, it is because he recognizes an analogy between Israel and Jesus, who repeats Israel's history but overcomes: for instance, tested forty days in the wilderness (as Israel was for forty years), Jesus passes the very temptations Israel failed (note the context of the verses he quotes from Deuteronomy).

The whole Old Testament bears witness to Christ because it reveals God's character, his way of saving by grace, his ways of using deliverers, his principles for atonement, covenant and promise, his purposes for his people, and so forth. This means that understanding it properly leads us to recognize in Christ the promised deliverer, and God had all this in mind when he inspired the Old Testament Scripture.

It does not mean, however, that we are free to come up with new "fulfilments" of Scripture randomly; the writers of the New Testament were guided by special inspiration, but we cannot make the same claim. That is not to deny that we should be led by the Spirit in understanding Scripture. It is rather to claim that if we say, "The Bible says," we dare say only what it specifically says. If we read into the Bible what is not there, we should be honest and say, "This is my view, not the Bible's," or "I felt as if God were leading me this way." The safest way to read Scripture is to look for its one meaning; with so much of the Bible yet to understand correctly, we have no reason to go looking for "hidden" meanings!

(5) We should beware of "prophecy teachers" who claim that every detail of the biblical text is being fulfilled in our generation.

Through most of church history and especially in the past two centuries, many interpreters have reinterpreted biblical prophecies to apply them to their own generation. Every decade or two, as news events change, they have to revise their interpretation of Scripture. In such cases teachers are not reading

Scripture on its own authority, but interpreting it in light of current news reports. This is problematic because they do it on two assumptions: first, that all prophecy applies to the final generation (which is not true, biblically); and second, that we must be the final generation. But most generations in history believed they were the final generation! God says that for all we know we might be--or we might not (Mk 13:32); we must always be ready (Mk 13:33-37). In the New Testament, the "last days" included the entire period between the first and second coming, including the first century (Acts 2:17; 1 Tim 4:1; 2 Tim 3:1; Heb 1:2; James 5:3; 2 Pet 3:3).

Most interpreters who claim, "All this is being fulfilled now" use biblical texts that are general enough to have been "fulfilled" similarly many other times. A number of books (e.g., Richard Kyle, *The Last Days Are Here Again* [Baker, 1998]) survey the history of errors that are common to *every* group that has practiced prophecy interpretation. Most people know that some groups repeatedly predicted the end of the world and were wrong, but we mostly know about those groups that kept insisting they were "somewhat" right. Yet from some early church fathers through some Reformers and many modern prophecy teachers, the same mistake has occurred over and over again. We should learn from history, as well as from Jesus' warnings (Mk 13:32; Acts 1:7).

Chapter 7
Revelation

Revelation is a particular kind of prophecy; because of its special importance and the interest it generates, I have devoted an entire section to its discussion. Revelation is a mixture of prophecy and apocalyptic (a special kind of prophecy that appears in Daniel, parts of Isaiah, Ezekiel, and Zechariah), delivered in a letter format.

On any book like Revelation, there will be serious differences of opinion, and we must be charitable in our disagreements. Nevertheless, it is worth exploring to see what the methods introduced above can teach us, and how they can take us beyond many of the views that have circulated widely. Reading Revelation as a whole (paying attention to whole-book context) and in light of its background (Old Testament and other background) will help us avoid or correct many of the common mistakes we have often inherited from others.

Revelation is not meant to be an obscure book. It may not be meant to satisfy our curiosity regarding all end-time details, but it certainly is a very practical book that presents God's demands on our lives. Thus it opens by promising a blessing to those who heed and obey its message (Rev 1:3)—which presumes that we can at least understand enough of it to obey it! An angel told Daniel that the book of Daniel would be sealed up and understood only in the end-time (Dan 12:9); by contrast, the angel told John not to seal up his book, because the end-time was near (Rev 22:10). Revelation may be "hidden" to those who think they need a special key in someone's teaching to unlock it. It is certainly unclear to those who interpret it only in light of current newspaper headlines—which require us to readjust our interpretations every year or two. But it is not as hidden to those of us who read Revelation straight through and understand it in its whole-book context. All Scripture should be profitable for teaching and instruction in righteousness from the time it was written (2 Tim 3:16-17)—so whatever else it might mean, at least Revelation must mean something relevant for our lives today.

A History of Misinterpretations

Too often people in the past two centuries have used "newspaper hermeneutics" to understand Revelation—that is, they have interpreted it in light of newspaper headlines. This is why many prophecy teachers have to change their interpretations of the book so often. That they recognize that Jesus could be coming soon, hence that prophecy is being fulfilled now, is commendable, but assertions that some current event definitely fulfills a biblical passage only leads to disillusionment when today's headlines end up in tomorrow's trash bin.

One example of newspaper hermeneutics involves interpretations of the "kings of the east" in Rev 16:12. In the early twentieth century, many North American interpreters thought of the "kings of the east" as the Ottoman Empire, headquartered in Turkey. Of course, the seven churches of western Asia Minor could never have conceived of kings of the "east" as Turkey, since Asia Minor is modern Turkey! But to western interpreters over a century ago, the Turks seemed the most threatening "eastern" empire on their horizon. After the Ottoman Empire was dismembered at the end of World War I, the new threatening "eastern" empire was imperial Japan (an empire that also threatened Korea, China, the Philippines and the rest of Asia). After imperial Japan was defeated at the end of World War II, western interpreters shifted the title to Communist China.

The only common factor in any of these interpretations was that these hostile kings were to the "east" of those interpreting the passage; sometimes the interpretations may also reveal some anti-Asian sentiments, which are unbiblical and ungodly. How would John's first readers have understood "kings of the east"? To everyone in the Roman Empire, and especially in Asia Minor, the greatest military threat was the Parthian Empire. The Parthian king rode a white horse, and claimed to be "king of kings and lord of lords." The definitive boundary between the Roman and Parthian empires was the River Euphrates (cf. 9:14; 16:12). Although they ruled in the region of Iran and Iraq, the geography is less important than the image: the most feared enemies of the Empire would invade it. In the end, it was northern barbarians rather than an eastern empire that did the Roman Empire in, but Rome did die by invasion. Yet conquest remains a frightening warning of judgment in any generation, and from any location (6:1-4).

Other prophetic interpretation errors abound. Jehovah's Witnesses, a cult, wrongly predicted Christ's return or other end-time events for 1874, 1878, 1881, 1910, 1914, 1918, 1925, 1975, and 1984 . Even Bible-loving Christians, however, have made mistakes in setting dates, contrary to our Lord's teaching (Mk 13:32). The church father Hippolytus concluded that the Lord would come by the year 500. Saint Martin of Tours believed that the Antichrist was already alive in his day; Martin died in 397, so if the final Antichrist is still alive, he possesses remarkable longevity!

Others have offered "prophetic" interpretations of the news uncritically. Some prophecy teachers in the 1920s embraced a work called *The Protocols of the*

Elders of Zion as confirming their teaching; the work is now known to be a forgery used by the Nazis. Many Christians in the 1970s worried about a computer in Belgium called "the beast"—unaware that the computer existed only in a novel! Around 1980 I heard a prophecy teacher explain that the Soviet Union would, in the next year or two, invade Iran, take control of the world's oil supply, and precipitate a world war. Needless to say, his prediction is running behind schedule at best.

Various books (including Richard Kyle, *The Last Days Are Here Again* [Baker, 1998]; Dwight Wilson, *Armageddon Now! The Premillenarian Response to Russia and Israel Since 1917* [Grand Rapids: Baker, 1977]) have documented countless claims made by prophecy teachers through history, and especially in the past 150 years, about various contemporary events. These teachers were occasionally right (about as often as astrologers), but were wrong the vast majority of times.

Below is a brief sampling of mistakes in recent history, borrowed from the introduction to my own commentary on Revelation (*Revelation*, NIV Application Commentary [Grand Rapids: Zondervan, 2000]):

• Christopher Columbus voyaged to the New World hoping to help precipitate the biblical new heaven and earth

- During the Reformation, Melchior Hoffman allowed himself to be arrested in Strassburg on the belief that it was about to become the New Jerusalem
- Also during the Reformation, Thomas Müntzer aided the Peasant's Revolt of 1524, believing that it would precipitate the final judgment; the peasants lost, and Müntzer was executed. In those days, end-time speculations died hard—sometimes literally!
- When King James I persecuted early Baptist leaders in England they feared that they were enduring the final tribulation
- Many Americans believed that King George III (probably one of England's most pious rulers, as John Wesley recognized) was the final Antichrist
- Many northern ministers expected the U.S. Civil War to establish God's kingdom in their favor; some southern ministers expected God to weigh in on the opposite side
- William Booth, an apostolic leader in the late nineteenth century whose Salvation Army was doing great works for God, believed that the Salvation Army he had founded "had been chosen by God as the chief agency to finally and fully establish" God's kingdom

More recently, in Christians in the U.S. bought over 3 million copies of Edgar Whisenant's *88 Reasons Why the Rapture Could Be in 1988*. A friend of mine worked in a Christian bookstore whose owner urged her to sell as many copies of the book by the end of 1988 as possible; the owner warned that no one would buy the book in 1989. Sure enough, Christians failed to buy many copies of his updated version the next year, rescheduling Jesus' return to 1989. Let it never be said that North American Christians are easily deceived—at least, twice in a row by the same author the following year. The world was watching, however: the campus newspaper at the university where I was doing my Ph.D. mocked the failed predictions. Others predicted the Lord's return for various dates in the 1990's or for the year 2000. As one other writer has pointed out, all predictors of times and seasons have had only one thing in common: they have all been wrong.

Often interpreters have proceeded on the basis of two assumptions: first, that we are the last generation; and second, that all prophecies apply to the last generation. The first assumption is always possible, but we cannot ever assert it dogmatically; every generation, looking at potential "signs" around them, has hoped that it might be the last generation. (Biblically, the last generation needs to do more than hope: we need to finish the task of world evangelization, whatever the cost.) The second assumption is simply wrong; many prophecies were already fulfilled within the Bible or await Jesus' return. Not all pertain specifically to the final generation before his return.

Views about Revelation

Traditionally, readers have taken one of the following approaches to interpreting Revelation:

1. Preterist: those who believe that everything was fulfilled in the first century
2. Historicist: those who believe that Revelation predicted the details of subsequent history which we can now recognize in history books.
3. Idealist: those who believe that Revelation contains timeless principles
4. Futurist: those who believe that Revelation addresses the future

The historicist interpretation has been largely abandoned because history does not fit the outline of Revelation very well. (This is true even for the letters to the seven churches, which some once read as stages of church history; very few scholars accept this today even in the "dispensational" tradition where it was once most common. Dispensationalism has also changed a great deal since it was founded.)

Of the other views, there is something legitimate in each, provided that we do not use one of them to exclude the other views. It is true that Revelation, like other books in the Bible, was written first to an ancient audience (the preterist view); the book explicitly addresses the seven churches in Asia Minor just like Paul addresses churches in his letters (Rev 1:4), and

Revelation is written in Greek and uses symbols that first-century readers would understand. This need not mean, however, that it does not speak about the future or (like the rest of the Bible) articulate principles useful for subsequent generations.

Revelation contains timeless principles relevant for the church in every generation. It also speaks about the future, in addition to the present and the past. Readers may disagree on how much of Revelation refers to the future, but almost everyone agrees that Revelation 21—22, at least, is future. Likewise, at least some of it refers directly to the past: the catching up of the child in Revelation 12 (whom most believe to be Jesus) has already happened.

Beyond these points, however, readers have come to startlingly different conclusions about Revelation's teaching throughout history. We can illustrate this divergence by way of commenting on the "millennium," the 1000-year period mentioned in Revelation 20. Many readers schooled in a particular tradition may be surprised to learn how many people they respect in church history have held other interpretations. That surprise offers some lessons for us: God does not use his servants solely on the basis of their end-time views, and we should always go back to the Bible to see what it teaches us. Just because everyone we know holds a certain view does not make it right; 150 years ago, most born-again Christians held a different view, and 100 years before that, a still different one.

After the Book of Revelation was finished, the first church fathers (leaders of the early church for the first few centuries) were premillennial; that is, they believed that Jesus would come back before the 1000 years in Revelation. They also were all post-tribulational; that is, they all believed either that they were already in the great tribulation, or that it was future but that Jesus would not return for his church until afterwards. But a few centuries later, by the time of Augustine, most Christians were amillennial. Many believed that when Constantine ended the persecutions against Christians, the 1000 years started, and many were expecting Jesus' return 1000 years after Constantine. Another amillennial view, more common today and easier to defend from Scripture, is that the millennium is symbolic for the period between the first and second coming, with Christ ruling until his enemies are put under his feet. Not only were most Medieval Christians amillennial, but so were most of the Reformers (including Luther and Calvin). Most denominations founded in times when amillennialism predominated are most amillennial today; the same is true of churches in various parts of the world founded by amillennial missionaries. By contrast, churches founded by premillennial missionaries are usually premillennial! John Wesley believed in two separate millennia in Revelation 20, one in heaven and the other on earth.

Most leaders of the Great Awakenings in the eighteenth- and especially nineteeth-century United States were postmillennial, including Jonathan Edwards and Charles Finney. During revivals that brought a large percentage of people in the early nineteenth-century United States to Christ, people exercised faith that "the gospel of the kingdom" would be "preached among all nations, and then the end will come" (Matt 24:14). Charles Finney, who may have led as many as half a million people to Christ, and helped lead the movement against slavery, was postmillennial. Postmillennialists believed that they would, through God's Spirit, establish God's kingdom on earth, and then Jesus would come back to take his throne. Today most Christians view postmillennialism as naïve optimism, but it was the dominant view of Christians in the U.S. in the nineteenth century.

Another view is first attested in the nineteenth and popular in the twentieth century. This view is called dispensational premillennialism. In or around 1830, John Nelson Darby came up with a system of interpretation that divided Scripture between what applied to Israel (the Old Testament, Gospels, Revelation, and much of Acts) and what applied directly to the church (especially the epistles). Through this system he argued that spiritual gifts were not for the church age, and that there would be a separate coming for the church (before the tribulation) and for Israel (afterward). Once introduced, the view was popularized through the Scofield Reference Bible, becoming popular especially in the early twentieth century. The failure of postmillennial optimism in the nineteenth century and the disintegration of the old, evangelical consensus in the U.S. made this view appear appealing. And after all, who would complain about getting raptured before a tribulation rather than afterward?

We cannot afford the space to debate for or against this view here, but merely wish to point out that most people who hold this view are unaware that no one in church history held this view before 1830. Some today believe that this view is clear; but Christians read the Bible for over 1700 years without anyone, so far as we know, noticing it! (And that, even though most Christians through history believed that they were already in the end-times, and many, like many Christians for the past few generations, that they were in the final generation.) Each view cites verses to defend its position, but each of these verses must be examined in context to be sure of its meaning. That includes views that are widely held today, like dispensationalism; and we should remember that such views widely held today were rarer or (in this case) unheard of in earlier history. For whatever it is worth, the majority of scholars committed to Scripture today are either amillennial or non-dispensational (generally post-tribulational) premillennial, though there are good scholars with other views.

In my opinion, premillennialists have an easier time explaining Revelation 20 itself, but amillennialists other end-time passages (for many, the debate then becomes whether to interpret the more explicit but single text in light of the many but less explicit ones, or the reverse). Since we will all know which view is correct by the time it happens, I see little point in arguing about it. Certainly it is foolish to break fellowship with other Christians over these matters! Why then do I raise the issue? Only to help us be more charitable to those who hold different interpretations of Revelation than we do. If we fight with our brothers and sisters over every single passage we interpret differently, then we will be out of fellowship with most of Christ's body. The true church is united on the essential matters necessary for following Jesus, but beyond that it is our unity and love that shows the world God's character (John 13:34-35; 17:20-23).

The real issues for us here must be the practical ones that our methods above can help us fathom. Some issues are very practical but no real Christian disputes them: for example, we all recognize that we must be ready for our Lord to return. But other issues are practical and often missed by interpreters who lack access to cultural background or whole-book context methods. Of these I offer a sampling below.

The Use of Symbolism?

Some people argue that we should take everything in the book of Revelation literally. But Revelation is full of images that we cannot take literally. Was a woman literally clothed with the sun in 12:1 (with the moon literally under her feet and twelve stars on her head)? Is Babylon literally the genetic mother of every prostitute in the world (17:5)? Revelation even tells us what some of its symbols represent, making clear that the book includes many symbols (1:20). God could create the sort of monsters described in Revelation 9, but they resemble locusts in Joel's prophecy, where they are simply a poetic description of either a locust invasion or an invading army (or a combination of both).

Then take as much as possible literally, comes the reply. But why should this be the case? Is it not better to be consistent with how we interpret the rest of Revelation, which clearly has many symbols? The appropriate way to read narratives is normally to read them literally, but as we noted above, that is not the best way to read Hebrew poetry, nor the Old Testament prophecies given in poetic form. Neither is it the way to read New Testament prophecies that use the same mode of symbolic communication as many

Old Testament prophecies. Some statements may be literal (we argue that the seven churches are, for example, literal churches), but others (like the woman clothed with the sun) are not, far more often than in narrative. Some scholars, pointing to a Greek word for "signified" or "communicated" in Rev 1:1, even suggest that one of the very terms used for revealing the message to John suggests that it came in symbols. (A related term for "sign" might bear this sense in 12:1, 3; 15:1.)

Jewish writers in John's day who imitated the writing style of Old Testament prophets (writing a form of literature later called apocalyptic) frequently used symbolism as well (for example, 1 Enoch portrays angels impregnating women as stars impregnating cows). Just as Jewish teachers often used riddles to provoke thought, apocalyptic writings used enigmatic prophecies to challenge the hearers. Even if we had only the Old Testament as background for Revelation, however, we would expect an abundance of prophetic symbolism (for example, see especially Zechariah, Ezekiel, and many prophecies in Daniel and Isaiah).

Whole-Book Context

Revelation offers a running contrast between two cities: Babylon and the New Jerusalem. Babylon is a prostitute (17:5); the New Jerusalem a bride (21:2). Babylon is decked out with gold and pearls (17:4), like a prostitute seeking to allure us with its offer of sinful, temporary gratification. The New Jerusalem is built of gold and its gates are pearls (21:18, 21). No one with any sense would prefer Babylon to the New Jerusalem; but only those with faith in God's promise wait for the city from above and resist present temptation.

In the days of Augustine (a North African theologian, AD 354-430), Rome fell to northern barbarian invaders, and Christians were dismayed. Augustine contrasted Rome with the City of God; earthly cities and empires decked with splendor will perish, but God's city is eternal, and his promise to us will never fail. The world demands that one take the mark of the beast, if one wishes to buy or sell (13:17). But for those who refuse to compromise with the world's kind of food (2:14, 20), God offers a promise of eternal food (2:7, 17) and manna even when the world persecutes them (12:6). Those who think themselves rich may be poor in what matters (3:17), just as those who seem to be poor may be rich in what matters (2:9). Jesus offers the true gold of the New Jerusalem to those who trust him rather than in their worldly wealth (3:18).

What can we learn about the New Jerusalem? Some translations explain that the New Jerusalem is 1500 miles in every direction, including high (21:16); this would make it about 1495 miles higher than the world's tallest mountain, where the air is already thin hence difficult to breathe. Admittedly, God could change the laws of physics if he wanted to, but there is another clue that the specific measure given for the New Jerusalem offers a symbolic point: in a city 1500 miles (about 2400 km.), the wall is only 72 yards (about 80 meters).

The answer to the significance of these apparently disproportionate measurements comes when we read the verse in Greek, or in a very literal translation, or in the footnote in most other translations: the New Jerusalem is 12,000 stadia cubed, with a wall of 144 cubits. By the time a reader of the book of Revelation gets to chapter 21, they have seen these numbers before. Revelation 7:4-8 and 14:1-5 speak of 144,000 chaste male Jews, 12,000 from each tribe. Because "Jerusalem" in the Bible referred to the people (Jerusalemites) as well as the place, the connection here makes sense: here are the New Jerusalemites who stand on Mount Zion (14:1), the people who will live in the New Jerusalem! The city belongs to those who endured for it, those who were "chaste" (14:4) and did not sleep with the prostitute Babylon. Does this mean that only male Jews will live in the New Jerusalem? (If the numbers are literal, each of them would get over 15 square miles on the city's ground floor.) Will Gentile Christians have no home there? Quite the contrary!

The list of tribes in 7:4-8 resembles military census lists in the Old Testament, suggesting an end-time army here. Jewish armies were male, and many Jewish people expected an end-time army; some also expected this army to be chaste before the battle. Not surprisingly, Revelation speaks of this group having "overcome" or "triumphed" (15:2-4; cf. 14:3); the beast might overcome God's servants on a human level (11:7; 13:7), but they overcame by refusing to disobey the Lord who holds the final victory (12:11). But does Revelation mean a literal army of 144,000 Jews? One can interpret it this way, and it would make sense; after all, the Bible does speak of Jewish people turning to the Lord in the end-time (Rom 11:26). But in the context of Revelation, I believe that another interpretation fits better.

Revelation elsewhere speaks of those who are spiritually Jewish (2:9; 3:9). Likewise, in the ancient world lampstands (John's symbol for the churches in 1:20) are symbolic for Jewish faith. Sometimes a second vision or dream repeated the point of the first one (e.g., Gen 37:7, 9; 40:1-7), and the same is probably true here: in the next paragraph, this triumphant army of 144,000 Israelites turns out to be a numberless crowd from all nations (7:9-17). The promises given to this crowd in 7:15-17 are promises God made to Israel in the Old Testament; but by following Israel's king these Gentiles have been grafted into Israel's heritage and promises, hence are spiritually Jewish. Whole-book context clarifies the connection between these two paragraphs. Two chapters earlier, John "hears" about the lion from the tribe of Judah, a symbol Judaism used for the warrior Messiah. But when John turns, what he "sees" is a slain lamb—one who conquered by his own death (5:5-6). Now John "hears" about 144,000 (7:4), but when he turns what he "sees" is a numberless multitude (7:9), possibly of martyrs who have shared Christ's suffering.

This fits what the text itself says. The 144,000 are "the servants of God" (7:3)—a title which elsewhere in Revelation refers to all believers in Jesus (1:1; 22:3). Are there only 144,000 servants of God? Are all of them ethnically Jewish, and all of them male? Certainly only God's servants will inhabit the New Jerusalem, but God's servants include both Jewish and Gentile followers of Jesus. The New Jerusalem is for all those who trust in Christ (21:7-8, 14, 27), and offers the same promise this passage suggests for the Gentile Christians (21:4 and 7:17). Jehovah's Witnesses wrongly take the number (144,000) literally but the male Jewish part figuratively; many Christians take both elements literally; in the context of Revelation, however, both elements are probably symbolic, with a deeper message for the church than most Christians recognize.

Whole-book context also offers insight into what Revelation may mean when it mentions the mark of the beast. Should we preach about that by simply warning people to avoid something in the future, or does it have something to teach us in the present?

Against what most of us have been taught, a consistent reading with the rest of Revelation suggests that this mark may not be visible to people. Notice the other marks written on people in the book of Revelation. For example, believers will become pillars in God's future temple, and just as other ancient pillars had names inscribed on them, so we will have God's name and the name of the New Jerusalem inscribed on us (3:12; cf. 2:17). Forever God's and the lamb's name will be written on our foreheads (22:4), perhaps like a slave brand or some other kind of brand showing to whom we belong. Jesus comes back with a name written on his thigh (19:12-13, 16), perhaps so John could read his title in the vision. Babylon the great has a name written on her forehead (17:5), but just as Babylon is not a literal woman, we recognize that the inscription is part of the vision, not literally written on a woman's head.

Just like God placed a mark on the righteous in Ezekiel 9:4-6, so God seals the 144,000 to protect them during his judgments (Rev 7:3). As in Ezekiel, this is a mark that only God himself sees. Because there were no chapter breaks in the original Bible, the first readers would have readily noticed the contrast between the 144,000 and the rest of the world (13:16—14:5). Those who follow the beast bear his name (13:17); those who follow the lamb bear his (14:1). The beast, progeny of its master the dragon, has seven heads and ten horns (12:3; 13:1; 17:3, 7). But a second beast is a deliberate counterfeit of the lamb (compare 5:6): he has two horns like a lamb, but speaks the dragon's message (13:11). A small army of 144,000 follow the true lamb; the rest of the world (the army of which is at least 200 million, 9:16) follows the beast. Each follower has an identifying mark showing their loyalty, either to the lamb or to the beast. Whether those in the world need to see a literal mark showing who belongs to them or simply signs of allegiance, the preaching point is clear: we must be loyal to God's side, not the world's, no matter what the cost.

Background

John probably wrote this book while in exile (1:9) in the time of the Roman emperor Domitian. Domitian demanded that everyone worship his statue as if he were a god, and the early Christians refused to give it. This issue was most pressing in western Asia Minor, where the seven churches were; some of these churches already were facing persecution (2:9-10, 13; 3:9). The first audience of Revelation would have found its warning about worshiping the image of the beast (13:15) relevant for their own day! Some of the other churches, however, were compromising with the very world system that was killing their siblings elsewhere (2:14, 20; 3:2, 15-18).

The seven churches of Asia Minor (1:4) were an audience just as real as any church to which Paul wrote. The churches are in the seven most prominent cities of the Roman province of Asia, and are arranged in precisely the sequence that a messenger traveling from Patmos would deliver the letters. Many issues addressed (such as wealth and distasteful water in Laodicea) address precisely the issues we know were relevant to these particular churches. This is not to say that the message is relevant only for the church addressed; Jesus invites everyone to listen in on his message to each of the churches (2:7). But we learn from their example the same way we learned from the churches Paul addressed: we learn the background so we can understand what issues the inspired writer was really addressing.

We spoke above about Babylon. This need no more be a literal name than the false prophets' parents had literally named them "Balaam" or "Jezebel" in 2:14, 20. As most Christians through history have recognized, the Babylon of John's day is Rome. Everyone knew that Rome was a city on seven hills (17:9); Rome even had an annual festival called "Seven Mountains," celebrating its founding. The imports in 18:12-13 are precisely the imports we know were most prominent in Rome, and in John's day Rome was the only mercantile empire to rule the kings of the earth by sea (17:18; 18:15-19). Most importantly, Jewish sources (and probably 1 Pet 5:13) already called Rome "Babylon." This was because Rome, like Babylon, had enslaved God's people and destroyed the temple.

Jewish people in the first century understood the fourth of Daniel's four oppressive kingdoms, which started from Babylon, to be Rome.

The implications of associating Revelation's "Babylon" with Rome are dramatic. In 18:2-3, John hears a funeral dirge over Babylon (just like the dirge over literal Babylon in Is 21:9). Rome, the mightiest empire the world had yet known, seemed ready to crush the tiny church of Jesus Christ. Rome had exiled the aged prophet John to the island of Patmos (1:9). Yet John hears a funeral dirge over this mighty empire! What faith it must have taken the early Christians to believe this promise that their oppressor would fall; yet John stood on the shoulders of earlier prophets who had prophesied against Assyria, literal Babylon, and so forth, and their prophecies had come to pass. Assyria, Babylon, Rome, and all the other empires of past history now lie in ashes. But the church of Jesus Christ, whom past empires threatened to stamp out, is more widespread than ever before! In a day when the church was established mainly in a few cities of the Roman Empire, John prophesied a church from every tribe and people and nation (5:9; 7:9)—and so it has come to pass!

But while "Babylon" for John's first readers is Rome, that is simply because Rome filled the role in John's day. Revelation 13 blends pictures of all *four* of the kingdom beasts of Daniel 7, creating a composite picture of evil empire in general. If Rome could be a new Babylon, there could be other new Babylons or new Romes, other evil empires that usurp the rightful role of God's future kingdom. These need not be geographically in Italy any more than Rome as a new Babylon was geographically in the Middle East. In other words, Babylon is the city of the world, like the city called "Sodom" and "Egypt" in 11:8; the world system, in its rebellion against God, is the alternative to the New Jerusalem. But just as the first Babylon fell, just as Rome fell, so likewise the other Babylon's and Rome's of history will fall. The final empires will collapse in the day when the kingdom of this world becomes the kingdom of our God and of his Christ (11:15)!

The Roman background might be relevant for understanding the evil king in Rev 13:1-3 and 17:10-11. The first emperor to officially persecute the church was Nero, who burned Christians alive as torches to light his gardens at night. When Nero was killed, however, the belief that he was coming back became so widespread that some impostors rose up claiming to be Nero; a few years before Revelation was written, one false Nero even persuaded the Parthians to follow him across the river Euphrates to invade Asia Minor. Many scholars thus suggest that the head wounded to death and returning to life in 13:3 is a "new Nero." This does not mean that he is literal Nero come back (any more than the figures in 11:3-6 are a literal Moses or literal Elijah come back); it would simply mean that he comes "in the spirit and power" of Nero (cf. Lk 1:17), i.e., he is being compared with Nero, the terrible persecutor. That is, Revelation uses the language of its day to say, "the future dictator will be like Nero Caesar, just as evil and persecuting Christians just as much." A Parthian invasion from across the Euphrates was a horrifying image in John's day, and a new Nero warned of future suffering.

Two further factors support this association with Nero. Revelation speaks of a past king not currently reigning, who would return (17:10-11); Nero was definitely one of the few kings before the current one when Revelation was written. Further, if his name is spelled in Hebrew letters, it comes out to 666. Many early Christians thought that Nero would return as the final Antichrist. There are, of course, other possible interpretations; "beast" in Hebrew letters also comes out to 666, and this point is no less relevant. Whether Nero or not, the final evil world ruler will be a wicked one! And the character of that evil ruler is already at work in others who do evil (2 Thess 2:7; 1 Jn 2:18). Let us never underestimate evil—nor forget that in the final analysis, the righteous God is still in control (Rev 17:17).

Other Reapplications of Old Testament Images

We noted above that the lion turns out to be a lamb. We could also note the reapplication of the plagues of Exodus in Revelation's judgments (chapters 8, 9, and 16), or the city called "Sodom" and "Egypt." Revelation is not pretending to "predict" the plagues of Moses' day, nor is the city of which it speaks the literal Sodom or Egypt of old (as if it could be both!)

In Revelation 21:16, the New Jerusalem's height is equal to its breadth and length—that is, it is shaped like a cube. This probably evokes the holy of holies in the Old Testament, which only the high priest could enter, and only once a year. In the New Jerusalem, however, all of us who believe in Jesus will be in God's full presence, as in the most holy place, without any barriers (a glory that our current mortal bodies could not withstand, but we will have glorified bodies then!) God's tabernacle will be among us, and he will dwell with us, and we will be his people (21:3).

Ezekiel prophesied a glorious new temple, with a river of water flowing from the temple, and fruitful trees on either side of the river (Ezek 47). Yet Revelation declares that there is no temple in the New Jerusalem (Rev 21:22). This is not to say that Revelation contradicts Ezekiel; instead, Revelation speaks of a greater reality to which Ezekiel's symbolism pointed. Ezekiel was showing that the future temple would be more glorious than the old temple. Revelation's promise is not less than Ezekiel's, but more: God and the lamb are the temple (21:22), and the river flows from their throne (22:1). The river is the river of life (22:1), and Ezekiel's trees are the tree of life (22:2). These new details point to a greater promise than Ezekiel's, by alluding back to Genesis. The original Eden had a river and tree of life, but was marred by a curse; the New Jerusalem has a river and tree of life, but no more curse (22:3). Paradise will be in God's presence forever and ever.

God's presence is not just a promise for the future New Jerusalem, but also for believers in heaven. Examine the furnishings of heaven in Revelation's scenes of it: for example, the ark (11:19); an altar of sacrifice (6:9); an altar of incense (8:3-5; 9:13; 14:18); lamps (4:5); a sea (15:2); and harps (5:8; 14:2; 15:2). How is heaven portrayed? It appears like a temple (the Old Testament temple had all of the above-mentioned furnishings). Thus it is not surprising that we find people worshiping in heaven; Revelation portrays it symbolically as a temple to remind us of our main activity there. We are never as close to heaven on this earth as when we worship God, an activity we will continue in a purer and fuller way in his presence forever.

In 6:9-11 we read of souls "under the altar," martyrs who died to spread the message of Jesus. Why are they "under the altar"? The blood of some sacrifices was poured out at the base of the altar in the Old Testament (Lev 4:7). These servants of God, by dying for the gospel, share in Christ's sufferings. As the lamb in 5:5-6 was sacrificed, so these servants of Christ have become living sacrifices with him.

Let us take one more example, perhaps the most controversial one possible, namely, the length of Revelation's tribulation. Are the 1260 days (11:2-3; 12:6, 14; 13:5) literal or figurative? Whether they are literal or figurative, several factors warn us not to assume, before investigating, that Revelation *must* mean them literally. Revelation gets this length of time from similar figures in Daniel (e.g., Dan 7:25; 12:7, 11); but it may address a different issue than Daniel does. In Daniel, this period involves an abomination of desolation (Dan 11:31; 12:11); Jesus shows that at least one of these happened before Revelation was written, within the generation Jesus spoke of it (Matt 24:15, 34; Mk 13:14, 30). (Those who claim that "generation" means "race" there are making up their own meanings for Greek words; the term always means "generation" in the Gospels.)

Daniel's literal abomination had already been fulfilled before Revelation was written (Revelation was written over two decades after the temple's destruction!) Further, Daniel's chronology rests on a symbolic reapplication of Jeremiah's "70 years" prophecy, after the 70 years were nearly over (Dan 9:2-3, 24). If Daniel could symbolically reapply a number in

Jeremiah, why could not Revelation reapply a number in Daniel? Many of John's Jewish contemporaries also reapplied Daniel's period of time symbolically, so everyone would have understood this method if Revelation followed it.

This would not mean that Daniel was not literal on this point (as we said, at least one of Daniel's abominations was fulfilled literally before Revelation was written, according to Jesus); only that Revelation applies the number differently. Because Revelation often uses numbers (like 12,000 and 144) symbolically, it is possible that Revelation borrows Daniel's number to tell us less about the *length* of time than the *kind* of time. But so far we have only argued that it is possible, not that Revelation actually uses the period symbolically. How can we know whether it employs the number symbolically or literally?

In Revelation 12:1-6, the dragon (the devil) opposes a woman and the child born from her. When the child is caught up to rule the nations with a rod of iron, the woman fled into the wilderness for 1260 days. Almost everyone agrees that the child refers to Jesus (cf. 12:17; 19:15); if so, the 1260 days seem to start when Jesus was exalted to heaven (over 60 years before Revelation was written). It begins with the first coming and ends with the second coming. For Judaism, the final tribulation was the period directly before the end (sometimes three and a half, or seven, or forty, or even 400 years), but we Christians recognize that we are already in the end-time. The coming Messiah has already come once, and we who live between the first and second coming live in the end-time, always awaiting our Lord's return. Just as the lion is the lamb, Christ's going and return frame the tribulation; all Jewish expectations take on new meaning in light of Christ's coming.

It is perfectly likely that there will in fact be further intensification of tribulation just before the end, but Revelation's point, at least in this passage, has a broader relevance to us than that. Our present time in the world is a time of tribulation, but we can take courage, because Jesus has overcome the world (Jn 16:33). The woman and her other children were in the wilderness (12:6, 17), which tells us about the nature of the in-between time. Israel lived in the wilderness between their redemption from Egypt and their inheritance in the promised land. By Christ's exaltation we, too, have begun to experience salvation; Satan can no longer accuse us (12:10); but we must still endure in this world until Christ's return (12:11-12).

There is not space here to address whether this is the only sense of the tribulation period in Revelation (I address the issue at greater length in relevant passages in my commentary on Revelation). But the *present* "end-time" does appear to be the point in chapter 12, and the New Testament often does view the present age as the end-time period. Ever since the first apostles, we have been in the "last days" (Acts 2:17; 1 Tim 4:1; 2 Tim 3:1; Jms 5:3; 1 Pet 1:20; 2 Pet 3:3). Jewish people spoke of the end-time as the "birth-pangs of the Messiah," but Jesus taught that the birth pangs have already started, whereas the end will come only when we have finished our mission of preaching the gospel to all nations (Matt 24:6-8, 14). Paul declared that even creation is already experiencing birth pangs with us to bring forth the new world (Rom 8:22-23). Knowing that we live in the end-time should affect how we live. Since Pentecost we have lived in the era of the outpouring of the Spirit; we live in an era begun by Jesus and to be finished by him. Therefore we should keep focused on who sent us, what our mission is, and what and whom we are really to be looking for.